Crime or Compassion?

One woman's story of a loving
friendship that knew
no bounds

Gail O'Rorke was born and raised in Crumlin, Dublin. She left school at an early age and was the mother of two children by the age of twenty. She married her lifelong partner Barry at the age of twenty-one and has lived in Tallaght since 1990.

She comes from a turbulent background and overcame many obstacles in her early years. She worked in a variety of cleaning jobs, one of which led her to meet a lady named Bernadette Forde who was a sufferer of Multiple Sclerosis. The loyalty and love of friendship that ensued resulted in her being the first person in the history of Ireland to be charged with the crime of assisting a suicide.

After many years of fear and worry, she was acquitted on 28 April 2015 at the Central Criminal Court of Justice, after a gruelling three-week trial. She continues to be an advocate for the right to die with dignity campaign. She now enjoys life surrounded by her partner Barry, their two grown children and their three grandchildren.

Crime or Compassion?

One woman's story of a loving
friendship that knew
no bounds

GAIL O'RORKE

HACHETTE
BOOKS
IRELAND

First published in 2017 by Hachette Books Ireland

Cataloguing in Publication Data is available from the British Library
ISBN 978 1 473 64985 9
Typeset in Palatino by redrattledesign.com

Printed and bound in Great Britain by Clays Ltd, St Ives plc

Hachette Books Ireland policy is to use papers that are natural, renewable and recyclable products and made from wood grown in sustainable forests. The logging and manufacturing processes are expected to conform to the environmental regulations of the country of origin.

Hachette Books Ireland
8 Castlecourt Centre
Castleknock
Dublin 15, Ireland

A division of Hachette UK Ltd
Carmelite House, 50 Victoria Embankment,
London EC4Y 0DZ, UK
www.hachettebooksireland.ie

For Barry
and
in memory of Bernadette Forde

Preface

In April 2015 I was tried and acquitted for the assisted suicide of my close friend – a woman for whom I also worked as a carer – Bernadette Forde. It was the first such case to ever be tested in Ireland, under the Criminal Law (Suicide) Act 1993.

Bernadette was in the late stages of multiple sclerosis, a gruelling disease from which she had suffered for over ten years. She had decided that she wished to end her life, on her own terms, with dignity. I, among others of a close-knit circle of loved ones, supported her choice.

Witnessing the decline of the health of someone you love, and the loss of dignity that can come as things they once took for granted fall away, is a humbling experience. The human impulse is to support them however needed, by whatever means necessary. It is an impulse that comes from love.

At the end of the day, a person can only tell their own story. Although Bernadette's circle of support contained a wider cast than me – loving people whom she trusted and appreciated – it is not my place to tell anyone else's story in this book.

Instead, I simply want to share a defining experience, and one that many will no doubt identify with aspects of: supporting someone you dearly love as they make a choice that causes those around them heartache, but that you know is right for them nonetheless.

In these pages I also tell the story of something that I would never wish on my worst enemy: being tried for a crime that I did not commit (yet at one point would have, not knowing the risks I was taking) – from the world-shattering moment when you are told that you are being charged, to the enduring fear of conviction, of spending up to fourteen years incarcerated, separated from those you love, and the toil of a trial in front of the eyes of the world – and its gruelling effects on your mental and emotional wellbeing. The might of the state fighting you, with your very freedom on the line. And then there is the acquittal – a victory, which is perhaps experienced less as a triumph than as the ultimate survival, and the most joyous of reliefs.

Finally, I tell of my younger years, surviving growing up in poverty in Dublin, in an abusive household, an experience that defined me in the choices I would make in my own later life, determined upon a course of love and caring, surrounded by good people.

The title of this book – *Crime or Compassion?* – illustrates the kernel of the complex issues surrounding assisted suicide. The will to assist comes only from a good place, yet ultimately, as things stand in Ireland, it is a crime, and a serious one. I hope that in some small way the outcome of my case will change things for the better for people in the future who make the choice, facing grave illness, to end their life with dignity – and their loved ones supporting that choice.

Yet if I was to go through it all again, I would not change anything. I was there for my friend when she needed me. I did my best for her, and knowing that she got her wish means more to me than I can ever say. Bernadette may have been a shadow of her former physical self by the time she died, wheelchair-bound and unable to carry out even the most simple of tasks that she felt gave her life quality. But when I think of her now, I see her as I imagine she is: dancing in heaven. This book is dedicated to the memory of Bernadette Forde.

1

I arrived into this world on 14 May 1971, the fifth and youngest child of Maud and Arthur Sinclair. I was born in the Coombe maternity hospital in Dublin. I almost didn't make it because it hadn't been noticed until nearly too late that my umbilical cord was wrapped around my neck. Thankfully a well-timed change in nursing staff brought a less tired and fresher nurse to care for my mother, and she quickly became aware of the dire situation. An emergency caesarean section was then performed which saved my life.

My father always said I was like a little monkey when I was born: long, yellow, and covered in fuzzy hair. For some reason there are no photos of me as a baby, in fact, I could count on one hand the number of photos taken of me during my childhood. I have one sister, Linda, who is six years older than me, and three brothers, Paul, Steve and Dave, who are ten, eleven and twelve years older respectively. We lived at 207 Windmill Road in Crumlin, a working-class area. It was the sort of place where everyone knew everyone, whether you wanted to or not, and our neighbourhood had an array of colourful characters, to say the least.

We were quite poor growing up because my father was unemployed for almost all of my childhood. In the 1970s and the beginning of the 1980s my father worked as a taxi driver but he lost his licence after he had a stroke. He took to his bed for almost a year and when he tried to get back to work, the carriage office in Dublin wouldn't renew his licence. Unfortunately, he had no other skills to fall back on, so he had to go on the dole.

We had enough to eat but with five children, food never lasted too long. On a good week it would last just four or five days. New shoes and the like were a luxury and my memories are of shoes with great gaping holes in the soles that constantly let the water and stones through. Because I was embarrassed about my poverty I modified a particular type of walk so that people walking behind me couldn't see under my feet. Cutting shoe-shaped cardboard cuttings from cereal boxes to serve as a temporary lining was a regular occurrence. We had no heating, had to put up with draughty old rotten windows and always wore hand-me-downs. Strangely, though, I wouldn't change any of these experiences for the world. Where I came from and the struggles I went through made me the strong person I am today.

I attended St Agnes' primary school on Armagh Road in Crumlin and then Rosary College secondary school, which was on the same road. Like a lot of children, I wasn't a huge fan of school. It was the good old 1970s, when education was inflicted upon you, rather than being something that was encouraging and motivating. We were educated by the Sisters of Mercy but liked to call them the Sisters of No Mercy. The only two subjects I liked were English and PE. A love for gymnastics runs through our family and it was something I continued in after-school classes. I was grateful to have local friends to play with because it meant I could avoid being at home. In my young child's brain, I didn't fully understand this avoidance, but as I grew older the dots joined up and it all made a lot more sense.

Life at 207 Windmill Road was never what one could call normal. My earliest memories are of feeling great upset and anxiety. It was a house that could best be described as dark. Happiness was a rare emotion. I have lots of memories of sporadic happy times, little bursts of normality, but sadly these times were short-lived. My father was to blame for the majority of the negativity that soaked our home. When I was a child it was my mother I blamed, but as an adult I now realise that my mother became the woman she was as a result of the life she had to endure, being married to a man like my father. To use the term 'monster' for my father would not be an exaggeration. He was an extremely violent man with an uncontrollable and vicious temper. He lacked remorse or conscience. He actually never drank alcohol so therefore lacked the often-used excuse of being drunk while behaving like an animal. He was fully in his right mind when he was violent, which to me made him even more of a monster. He willingly, knowingly behaved in this vicious way towards the very people he was supposed to protect – his wife and children.

Being the baby of the family has meant that some things I know about are not from my own memory; they are from listening to my siblings talking about how things were. The extreme and severe beatings my mother endured for so many years reduced in number a few years after I was born and I was shielded from the ones that did occur by my sister as much as she could. I remember sitting on the stairs with Linda many times while she sang songs to me to drown out the noises coming from down below. 'Billy, Don't be a Hero' by Paper Lace, 'Ben' by Michael Jackson and 'Honey' by Bobby Goldsboro are the ones I particularly remember.

Because of the bigger age-gap between myself and my brothers, they were mostly at work, or socialising in their mid- to late teens, so I was truly blessed to have my big sis to mind me. For the most part the beatings my father gave my mother had stopped by the time I reached the age of about five or six. However, the emotional and psychological abuse continued. As younger boys, all three of my brothers experienced unbelievable abuse from our father. They received severe beatings from a very young age. My father even picked one of them up as a young baby and threw him the length of the living room. He once put a handgun in one of their mouths. It didn't take much to push him over the edge – it could be something as simple as coming back from the shop slightly short-changed. I felt he derived great pleasure from torturing and bullying everyone around him, and it greatly upset me when I heard these stories from my siblings. As a parent myself, it's impossible to comprehend such treatment towards anyone, let alone your own children. Individually, all five of us experienced different kinds of abuse from our father.

The beatings my mother endured were so extreme that there were times when she couldn't leave the house for weeks because of the severity of her injuries. As a result, she developed agoraphobia. She became so consumed with fear that she needed to take one or two Valium before leaving the house, even when going to the local shops. The other and more devastating effect the abuse had on her was that she became a tyrant in her own home. The intense pent-up aggression she felt towards my father turned into a weapon she used against all five of her children. She grew to be violent, manipulative and devious, and under no circumstances would she ever admit that she was wrong about anything. She was extremely difficult and devoid of any type of affection towards us. In all the years I lived under her roof, I received a total of two hugs: once when I got my first period at the age of eleven and the second when I returned from a camping trip aged sixteen.

After I was born, my mother developed breast cancer. I believe it could have been brought on by the extreme violence or just the sheer stress of living with my father. She had a mastectomy and chemotherapy and succeeded in overcoming the illness but in the end the cancer conquered her because she lived in fear of its return for the rest of her life. She became a hypochondriac and had a pill for every illness. For her it was the magic box of medicines that fixed most of life's little problems. I also feel that my mother's illness so soon after I was born more than likely affected the natural bonding between mother and baby.

The physical abuse was only one of the many dark attributes my father possessed. He was also a master of mind manipulation. When I was a child, I adored him. I followed after him like a little lapdog, and loved hanging around while he was doing odd jobs or working on old cars he mended for friends. You see, my father never hit me. He was fun to be around and would often take my side in arguments against my mother. Behind her back he would call her all sorts of names and tell me that she was nothing but an effing bitch. Of course I didn't know any better, so I agreed with him. Unbeknownst to my young, naive mind, my father's words and actions were all part of a more sinister intention.

As an adult, I fully understand and see the whole picture clearly but as a child I was blind to his grooming. Sadly, we lived in terribly ignorant times back then. These days children are much better informed, educated and aware of the darker side of society, and of what is and isn't acceptable. Unfortunately, in the 1970s and '80s abuse remained something with no name. My father consistently drove a silent, almost subliminal, wedge between me and my mother. He and I often sat excitedly making plans to bump her off, to get rid of her for good.

He was one of the founding members of a gun club and said that it could be easily done; my mother could have a little 'accident' at the gun range. Alternatively, he could run her over in the driveway and make it look like an unfortunate accident. I wasn't fazed by these plans. A huge part of me actually looked forward to a life without my mother. As I grew up, my hatred for her reached the point where I felt sick just looking at her. I know how cruel and horrible that sounds, but it was simply how I was schooled to feel. And as my father solidified this hatred towards my mother, I grew to love him more. Added to this, he was very lenient with me: for example, one of the things he allowed me to do was stay out late; being only about eleven or twelve, he knew I was impressionable and that silly things like this were important to a young girl wanting to seem more grown-up.

There was and still is the other side to my father, though thankfully these days he is too old and ill to be a threat to anyone. There was a reason he was my 'friend', a reason why he wanted me to trust him. It was always there but of course at the time I was blind to it. All I knew was that every day, for some reason, I felt sick, with a pain in my stomach and a tightness in my throat. I now know that what I am describing is anxiety, but at the time it had no name – it was just a feeling. As I got a little older, my father's behaviour towards me intensified. All my life he had been a grabber and a toucher but when I reached puberty my days became a constant bombardment of questions about my developing body. Absolutely nothing was sacred. He wanted to know everything in fine detail. I detested his questions and dreaded that 'trapped' feeling. I felt I couldn't just tell him to stop and walk away: he was my father and he was in charge and I had no choice but to stand there and listen and obey. I couldn't even talk to anyone else in the family about it. Segregation, separation and secrets were the foundations our house was built on. I now know that my sister Linda and brother Steve were experiencing all the same things, but back then I wasn't aware of this. My brother Paul has no childhood memories so can't say if he did or didn't, and Dave, the eldest, says that it never happened to him.

One night, when I was about thirteen, my father drove me into Dublin, down to the long wall at Guinness' brewery. The long-distance truck drivers used to park there to rest for the night. He told me that Linda worked there as a prostitute and that one day in the not-too-distant future I too would work there. He said it in such a matter-of-fact way that I don't think I even flinched. He also continually talked about how willing a participant my sister was in his dirty deeds. Of course it was all entirely fabricated, but it's what he wanted me to believe.

Every few weeks I would come home from school

and see him bursting into the living room, naked from the waist down, and telling me that he had just finished with Linda in the bedroom upstairs. She actually wasn't in the house at all, but I didn't know that at the time. He was trying to get inside my head. A consequence of this was that I grew to resent Linda. Why was she doing this? My young head was a mess.

Even in a room filled with people my father would brazenly ogle me and whisper dirty requests in my ear at any given opportunity. He loved talking dirty. He regularly sneaked into my room at night. I shared a room with my brothers, and whenever my father came in, I would move around loudly in my bed in an attempt to disturb one of the boys, so that my father would leave for fear of being discovered. He would sit silently beside my bed, remove the covers and attempt to touch me inappropriately, but my efforts at making noise were thankfully my best deterrent. I don't know if being the youngest made me less afraid of him and as a result made him more cautious but, whatever the reasons, he was less sexually heavy-handed with me than with some of my other siblings. However, there were many nights when I would wake up as he was leaving the room. Of these nights I have no other memories. Now I think that perhaps absent memories are a blessing. One's mind copes in ways we may never understand. My sister calls it 'our lion in the basement'. He may remain quietly sleeping for many years, she says, but one day he will scratch and bang on the door looking for release. My answer to this is that I will face my lion when that time comes; for now I choose to leave him undisturbed.

One of the side-effects of growing up in this type of environment was that I began to truly believe that my body was the one thing to offer the world of men. I suppose it was all a form of brainwashing and regretfully we lived at a time when there seemed to be many men around who were not unlike my father. Sometimes it felt as though there was a sign on my back advertising my level of desensitisation to abuse. It resulted in both Linda and I finding ourselves in dangerous situations throughout our teenage years, and experiencing traumatic events that we kept a secret from the world. Both of us in those years were the victims of rape but told no one about it, not even confiding in each other. Another unspoken dirty secret, I suppose. My father had his own warped philosophy: he always said that there was no such thing as rape. He reckoned a girl could run faster with her skirt around her neck than a man could with his trousers around his ankles.

Somehow, throughout my childhood I managed to duck and dive enough to avoid being in a situation where my father could have sex with me. I don't quite know how I did it, but I did. It was now 1987. I was sixteen and working full-time in a dry cleaners in Donnybrook. I was dating a young soldier from Saggart called Kevin and thought I was in love.

I couldn't wait to be free of my house and well away from the torments of my father and the craziness of my mother. I decided, like many troubled young people, that I was going to run away. I stayed in a women's refuge on the South Circular Road on the first night. I can't actually remember how or why I ended up there but it was terrifying. Being woken at all hours with a nun standing over my bed sprinkling holy water on me was scary! On my second night on the run I stayed in a flat on Emmet Road in Inchicore which belonged to a friend of Kevin's. I then stayed with a friend and her family in Ballyfermot for a couple of days. I remember my parents came knocking on her door looking for me, and I hid in an alcove behind the fridge listening to them showing fake concern for my whereabouts. I knew all they were worried about was that I would tell others our family's dirty little secrets. Thankfully, my friend lied for me and they went away. They must have had their suspicions because a day or two later the gardaí arrived at the door looking for me. I knew I had no choice but to come out of hiding and so I gave myself up.

I was driven to Crumlin Garda Station for an interview and was placed in a room which had a desk in the centre, a couple of chairs and a long glass wall on one side. I felt very alone and afraid. The guards began asking me lots of questions about why I had run away. Throughout the interview my father watched us from outside the room; he couldn't hear what was being said but he could see me clearly. He paced up and down, his hands behind his back, and glared at me with his emotionless eyes. I can't even remember the questions I was asked because I was too focused on him watching my every move. I was really terrified. But I know that I recounted what my father had been doing to me – the years of torment, constantly fending off his inappropriate advances and disgusting groping behaviour, the ongoing depravity we as a family had to endure. I honestly thought that if they knew, something would be done about it. But it wasn't to be, as I don't believe my father was even questioned – certainly, nothing ever came of my interview with the gardaí.

I later learned that while I was in the garda station, my mother was at home forcing my two siblings who were in the house at the time to their knees, making them place their hands on the bible and swear that nothing was going on.

Ultimately, nothing happened as a result of the testimony I gave the guards. I was clearly disbelieved by all involved. I was marched unceremoniously back to number 207 where, unsurprisingly, my mother didn't have a whole lot to say to me. But as long as I live, I will never forget the few words she uttered:

'You should have worn more clothes in bed.' What mother says something like that to their child? Maybe a mother who in her dark and tormented mind chose to offer up her children to the evils of my father and in the process be left alone herself.

Even then, I knew deep down that my mother was fully aware of what my father was up to with his children. She behaved in ways that were not normal. She was always telling Linda and me to 'fix' ourselves when he was around: 'Pull your skirt down', 'Fix your top', 'Don't sit that way in front of your father', and on and on.

Many years on from the night in the garda station, out of the blue I received a letter from the Health Service Executive, in which they apologised to me for how things had been handled back in 1987, when I had told the guards about my father. They offered support and counselling should I need it. I was around thirty at the time. As nice as the acknowledgment was, it was all far too late.

2

Over the next few months, I left my job in the dry cleaners and began working in Kentucky Fried Chicken in O'Connell Street. I was now seventeen. Even though my father had backed off significantly since my attempt to rat him out, he was still a threat. But he also knew the police were now aware of who he was and what he was up to, so he didn't take as many risks. Not one word was mentioned among the rest of my family about what had happened in the garda station. Everyone just went back to the familiar rule and role of secrecy. It was all we really knew.

I had also recently broken up with my boyfriend Kevin. After he returned from a tour in the Lebanon, I found out he had been cheating on me – and that was the end of that as far as I was concerned. One day, 20 June 1988, while returning from running some errands for my mother I had my head turned by the dull roar of a motorbike engine. I have always had a thing for bikes and instinctively turned to see where the sound was coming from. Outside one of the local shops were two figures. One was standing beside the bike and one was sitting on it. They waved, so I waved back. The guy sitting on the bike began to drive towards me. As he pulled alongside, he smiled and introduced himself as Paul. He looked foreign, with big brown eyes and long brown hair. I noticed he had a big cast on his leg and thought to myself that he shouldn't be driving a motorbike. However, being a little shy, I said nothing.

We chatted briefly and after a minute or two his companion made his way towards us. I can still see Barry as if it was yesterday: black leather biker jacket, a denim cut-off covered in colourful embroidery and lots of badges, tight, ripped pale denims and white runner boots. He was drop dead gorgeous and walked with a cheeky little swagger. I noticed his accent was rather posh, compared to what I was used to then. He told me his name, and that he was twenty years old and from Raheny on the northside of Dublin. With Paul motoring slowly on the bike beside us, Barry and I walked together towards my house, comfortably yapping away. When we reached my garden wall Barry asked if he could come back later that day to see me again. I was delighted. My stomach was doing somersaults of excitement, and of course I said yes.

The hours seemed to drag as I waited. Barry arrived back some hours later and we sat on the wall outside my house talking and laughing. We made sure we sat out of the watchful eye of my mother for I knew she wouldn't have approved of him, solely based on how he looked. From that first meeting I felt something very different about Barry, compared with my previous boyfriends. I couldn't as yet put my finger on it but deep down in my gut there was definitely something special going on between us. We talked and talked until regretfully it was time for me to go in for the night. Before he left, we made arrangements to meet up again the following day. We kissed a very long kiss goodnight and he headed off down Windmill Road back towards the caravan site he was staying in that night – at that time Barry was paling around with a group of bikers known as The Road Rockers who lived on the site. As I watched him walking away, he suddenly turned around and shouted at the top of his voice, 'Gail Sinclair, I love you!' The crazy thing was, he truly meant it and I believed him. I shouted back at him, 'I love you too!'

I floated back in to my house on a loved-up cushion of air. We had only just met but I knew that this man was going to be in my life for a very long time to come. I felt so safe and comfortable in his presence, which were two things greatly lacking in my life so far. My mother was not at all a fan of my new boyfriend. The minute she saw him, she judged him on his appearance, saying that he was a scruffy biker. She was also cripplingly envious of his family and couldn't bear to listen when I talked about them. Barry came from a family where the mother loved her children and the father worked very hard to provide for them, and they lived in a big five-bedroom house. Resentment oozed from my mother's every pore. But no matter what she said or however she attempted to split us up, it never worked. I had found a man who loved me for just being me, a man who protected me and made me feel secure, and I wasn't walking away from him for all the tea in China.

I remember after a few weeks of dating, I sneaked off to a motorbike rally with Barry. I lied to my mother, telling her I was going to see Michael Jackson live in concert in Cork. Unfortunately, my brother Paul was at the gig so when I returned she interrogated me about the songs and outfits Michael had worn. It didn't take long for her to find out the truth. She went bonkers. She dragged my new leather biker jacket off my back and threw it into the fire in a rage. I ran to get out of the house, but my parents ran to the front and the back of the house to block my exits. As my father ran towards the back, I grabbed my jacket from the fire and pushed my way past him, running down the road as fast as my legs could carry me towards the site where I knew Barry was spending some time with his friends. We sat in a damp caravan until eventually I spotted my father coming through the gate, looking for me. I was so embarrassed in front of all Barry's cool biker friends. All my father said was, 'Your mother wants to see you!'

I was terrified at the thought of facing her wrath but, as I stood to leave, Barry stood alongside me, taking my hand in his. He looked at me and said, 'Don't worry. I'll face your mother with you. I'll protect you'. A sense of relief washed over me but was mixed with terror because I knew how my mother would react when she saw him. We walked hand in hand, about ten feet behind my father. When we went in to the living room, my mother's face turned purple with rage when she saw that I wasn't alone. She never did like to air our dirty laundry in front of anyone and particularly in front of the scruffy biker with the lovely family. She didn't say much, but I'd say her mouth was filling with blood from biting her tongue so hard.

Her calmness terrified me because I knew that as soon as Barry left, I was going to be given a severe thrashing, verbally and physically. When it was clear that her rant was over, Barry said, 'I mean no disrespect, Mrs Sinclair, but I want to let you know that I'm not going away, so you'll simply have to get used to the idea of me being your daughter's boyfriend.' Holy shit! I thought. Did he just say that? Oh sweet Lamb of God, she's going to bury him in the back garden alongside our dead pets (including my hamster Mandy whom my father had shot in the head with a .22 rifle while I was at school because he didn't like the way she squeaked).

But no! She swallowed her bile with great difficulty in her attempt to be the 'better person'. Knowing how my mother's mind worked, there was no way she would give Barry any reason to talk badly of us to his perfect little family, so she put on her best fake face and tried hard to muffle the angry demon bubbling below the surface. As I'd expected, that night I received a few slaps and a barrage of verbal abuse, but only after all the windows had been tightly closed. God forbid the neighbours would hear the real mother she was.

Barry and I continued dating for the next few months and in late October I began missing my period. Since the age of eleven, my cycle was as regular as clockwork, so I knew something was amiss. We bought a pregnancy test and headed for a friend's house in Terenure. Back then, pregnancy tests took an hour to show the result. I did the deed and placed the test on the window ledge. Looking back, I'm sure I should have been more worried than I was, even a little scared, but I wasn't, not one tiny little bit.

A couple of minutes before the hour was up, Barry jumped up from his seat and sprinted up the stairs. Before I had time to catch up with him, he shouted from the bathroom at the top of his voice, 'I'm going to be a daddy, I'm going to be a daddy!' We were over the moon. Regardless of our joy, we now had to face telling my parents. I was only seventeen, Barry was twenty and we had only been dating for about four months. This had the potential to become very messy, but I didn't care.

We decided to tell Barry's parents first since it seemed the easier of two options. Barry's mother, Mai, just hugged the two of us and congratulated us. I'm sure deep down she was panicking. She hardly knew me but she put that to one side and made it a special moment about us and not herself. She was a remarkable woman and handled the situation with great tenderness.

Before we plucked up the courage to face my parents, we headed to London for three days, to get our heads together before the proverbial shit hit the fan. It was a lovely break away and much needed. When we returned, we went to my house and called my mother and father into the kitchen to deliver what

I knew would be devastating news to them. Three of my siblings had already had babies out of wedlock, a thing my parents had not been happy about, and now I, the youngest, was coming to them with the same news.

Barry and I stood united side by side in the tiny kitchen swallowing large gulps of air while attempting not to panic. When we told them, my mother looked disgusted but I had expected nothing else. She just threw us a filthy look, muttered something and left us alone with my father. All he asked was if we had travelled to London for an abortion. Once he was reassured that we hadn't, he just said, 'Fair enough', before also leaving the room. We left soon after. Barry and I had done our duty and told them. The relief was enormous. We could now resume feeling ecstatically happy about the new life growing inside me.

That Christmas Eve, Barry arrived over to my house for a visit. When he walked in, instead of coming to sit with me in the parlour he went into the living room to my parents. Minutes later, he joined me, and before I knew what was going on he got down on bended knee and proposed to me with a beautiful engagement ring. I burst into tears and agreed without hesitation. The reason for his brief detour was to ask my father for his permission to marry me. Regardless of the man my father was, Barry wanted to do it properly and with respect. I was over the moon and wore my beautiful new engagement ring with pride.

When I was about five months' pregnant, Barry's mother asked if I would like to come and live in her house. She knew all about life in 207 and understood how stressful it was for me. Being pregnant was enough to deal with without enduring the tension of living with my parents, who now had more reason to be harsh and difficult towards me. I jumped at the offer. But my mother hit the roof when I asked her. I pleaded, and eventually she agreed but only with the promise that I would return if Barry and I hadn't found a place of our own within two months. I would have agreed to anything just to escape. Once I got out of that house, there wasn't a snowball's chance in hell that I would return.

So here I was, very soon to be a mother. I just loved everything about being pregnant and was immensely proud of my ever-growing bump. In April 1989 we were offered a one-bedroom flat in Ballymun. We were chuffed. It didn't matter where it was as long as it was ours, so we grabbed it with both hands. As luck would have it, Barry's cousin Trish and her husband Richie lived in the next block of flats to us. Trish had been very close to Barry growing up, so it was great comfort having them so near. Trish too was expecting a baby around the same time as me, which drew us all even closer together.

In those days Ballymun was quite a rough area so we kept to ourselves. Outside our door was a rubbish chute overflowing with refuse, a lift that hardly ever worked – probably broken from transporting horses in it – and stairs that smelled of a combination of urine and excrement and which were in constant darkness because of broken light bulbs. But once we closed our red front door, none of that mattered. It was our little safe haven: me, my bump, my partner, and Midnight, our cat.

On 24 July 1989 at 11.25 a.m. our son Aaron Barry O'Rorke was born in the Rotunda hospital in Dublin, weighing in at 8lb 9oz after twenty-three hours of excruciating labour. He was perfect in every way and beautiful, with a thick mop of dark brown hair. Poor Barry cried for what seemed like hours. He was truly in love with his little boy, and it was a joy to witness such adoration. When we eventually managed to peel ourselves away from each other, Barry headed to my mother's house first to tell our news. Did she congratulate him? No! She went upstairs, dug out old love letters which my ex, Kevin, had written to me while in the Lebanon and made Barry sit while she read out Kevin's undying love for me. To this day I can't believe she did this. It really showed us how dark her mind was. All she wanted to do was to upset Barry and make him feel insecure. Thankfully, his next stop was his own mother's house where he received the hero's welcome he deserved.

I took to motherhood like a duck to water. Having a baby to nurture and the opportunity to provide him with a safe home and an environment bursting at the seams with love was the most beautiful of blessings. I know this will sound cheesy, but I truly felt that my angels had first sent me Barry and now our little boy. I was happier than I had ever been. Like most young families, money was quite tight, so we both needed to work to make ends meet. I got a job working in a dry-cleaner's in Blackrock while Barry worked as a security guard in Rialto. Barry's mother Mai took care of Aaron during the day. Every day was spent on buses and trains to and from work and Mai's house. I don't know how we would have coped without her support; she was amazing throughout those scary first few years. She adored Aaron. There was no other baby more special than her little grandson and she loved minding him. We were still visiting my parents, but the two-bus journey there and back, as well as a mile or so to walk from the bus stop, pushing a buggy, was a great excuse to call over less often. Besides, the visits invariably ended with a big argument about something or other, usually started by my mother. She could not keep her mouth shut, and was always happiest when upsetting someone.

In the spring of 1990 we received the news that a

council house in Jobstown, Tallaght was vacant if we were interested. Again, we were lucky: my brother Steve lived across the road from the house and, with the help of a good neighbour, Pat Waters, they secured it for us. I remember so clearly the day we moved in. We had nothing to call our own: no furniture, no carpet, and no curtains. That first night Barry and I slept on a mattress on the floor in the living room, shivering with nerves and the cold – Aaron was being minded by family while we got the place habitable and warm enough for a baby to be in.

Within two weeks of us moving in, we found out that we were expecting a second baby. It wasn't a shock because it was what we wanted: two children close together in age. Once more the pair of us were on cloud nine. Our little life was beginning to come together. I quit my job in the dry-cleaner's soon after hearing I was pregnant, to become a full-time stay-at-home mother. We were so happy with our growing little family and felt almost invincible together. Barry's parents called once or twice a week, often bringing groceries and other household necessities to help us along when we were struggling. We were still reluctantly visiting my parents but only every fortnight or so. When I look back, I could ask myself why on earth I continued to see them, but in all fairness it's not an easy thing to disown your own mother and father. There is an inherent emotional pull and a family guilt that is very hard to explain but that works at a deep level. I suppose, at the end of the day, we only have one family.

Our amazingly beautiful little daughter, Dawn Rhiannon O'Rorke, was born on 12 December 1990, weighing in at 8lb 4oz, and like her brother, she had a big mop of dark hair. A perfect little girl, she completed our family in a way I could only have dreamed of. A little girl to cuddle and dress like a little princess.

In June 1992 we were married at St Agnes' Church in Crumlin village, the same church where I was baptised, made my communion and was confirmed. Like all weddings, the run-up to the day was quite stressful. Money was very tight so it was all done on a small budget, but regardless of this we were both very excited.

I hired my dress from a shop in Talbot Street. It cost £210 to rent which at the time was a lot of money, but it was the one I had my heart set on. It's so funny when you look back on old photos of the day how outdated it seems, but at the time I felt like a princess when I tried it on. We had the reception in the Spawell Hotel in Templeogue. I remember the day as if it was only yesterday, though it wasn't without its sadness and heartache. Barry's mam had one sister, Patsy, who had been diagnosed with motor neurone disease a number of years previously. Anyone familiar with

MND knows what a truly awful condition it is. Patsy deteriorated to the point where she was no longer able to do anything for herself, even though her brain was fully functional. She passed away three days before our wedding and was laid to rest the morning we were married. Barry was always very close to his Auntie Patsy and having to go from her funeral, the saddest of days for his family, to his wedding, the most joyous of occasions, was unbelievably difficult. How Mai managed so soon after losing her only sister I will never truly know. Some of Patsy's grown children, who also came to our wedding, were amazingly strong.

While all this was going on, I, the bride-to-be, was in my mother's house getting ready to marry my soulmate and best friend. I remember my mother taking hold of my shoulders just as I was about to walk down the stairs towards all the neighbours and well-wishers who were waiting patiently in the hallway. She looked into my eyes and said, 'Gail, you don't have to do this, it's not too late.' I couldn't believe what she was saying. Wild horses wouldn't have stopped me from marrying Barry but as always my mother knew how to throw the proverbial spanner in the works. I looked into her eyes and simply said, 'Mam, I'm marrying him' before I walked down the stairs feeling like the most beautiful bride in the world.

The ceremony was so lovely. When standing on the altar I felt as though it was just the two of us in the church; it was magical. The service was performed by a priest named Bernard Simpson, who in the world of priests was rather young. He made it such a special day for the two of us and brought a rare sense of humour to proceedings. It was then off to the hotel for dinner, drinks and dancing. All in all it was an unforgettable day. We spent that night at a friend's house and headed off to London for a three-day honeymoon the following day. We had very little money but neither of us cared; as long as we were together that was all that mattered.

Over the next few years we had many ups and downs, some financial, some not. Mai was sadly taken from us by cancer at the age of fifty-eight. It had a devastating effect on all of us, but Barry really fell apart. He was as close as a son can be to a mother. My babies, although extremely fond of their grandmother, were a little too young to grasp the enormity of the loss. Soon after Mai's death, Barry's father Pat and his older brother Ray moved to Ballivor in County Meath and we saw less and less of them. In a family of boys, Mai had been the glue that had held them all together.

Our visits to my parents were becoming increasingly strained. We dreaded these occasions, and now that my babies were growing, I hated them being around my father. I knew he could not control his behaviour, so they stayed with me wherever I went while we were in the house. With the passing of time, our visits became even more infrequent. Things finally came to a head over the Easter weekend in 1995. My father was up visiting my brother Steve who lived across the road from us, with his then wife Sandra and their two daughters. He had brought Easter eggs for their children and he first visited Steve's before calling to my place with eggs for Aaron and Dawn. It was a short and uncomfortable visit. His attempt at niceness was skin-crawlingly sickening, a timid attempt to stay in my good books. Minutes after he left, a rage rose up inside me. I was furious that he had called to my home, and I just couldn't keep my emotions hidden anymore. I saw that he had gone back to Steve's before heading home. I'd had enough pretending to last me a lifetime, so I gathered up the eggs he had brought and marched across the small green between my house and Steve's. I knocked so hard on the door, I thought it might break.

When Sandra opened it, I pushed past her into the hall and threw the eggs at my father. I screamed at him that he was never to come near me, my children or my house again. Years of pent-up emotion poured from my mouth. He just stood there unsuccessfully attempting to interrupt me. With every angry word I shouted I felt better, lighter and stronger. When I had finished, I stormed out of the house trembling with fear but elated. Oh my God! I'd done it. I was finally free of my parents and it felt fantastic.

The following years were pretty uneventful. My father and mother were no longer in our lives. It is only when you are away from something so suffocatingly negative that you realise how much it has been affecting your everyday life. I continued to be a happy stay-at-home mother. Barry finished doing security work and became a motorbike courier. It was a dangerous and very stressful job but it paid the bills and kept our heads above water. Towards the end of 1998 the wife of one of Barry's courier friends, Elaine Byrne, offered me some part-time work doing a few hours cleaning houses. I jumped at the offer. The kids were now in school so I had the time during the day, and the extra money would greatly help us.

Throughout my life most of my jobs revolved around cleaning, be it in housekeeping in the Westbury Hotel or dry cleaning in Donnybrook. I have always been a bit of a clean freak, so I knew this new job at First Maids would suit me. It was while working there that I met someone who became one of my greatest friends. She was a young girl called Sinead Greene. We hit it off straight away and spent our days cleaning and laughing. She was and still is one of the funniest people I have ever met. It turned out to be a friendship that would stand the test of time and, although these days we don't see each other as often as we would like, she is still one of my closest and most-loved friends.

With the little extra money coming in, Barry and I decided to bring Aaron and Dawn to London for a short break. We had a great time, but during our stay we began to notice that Aaron's behaviour was a little out of the ordinary. He kept losing his balance and bumping into people and objects. I wasn't sure if it was just a nine-year-old acting the maggot, but it continued and was worrying. When we returned home, we also noticed a physical change in Aaron. The right side of his little face was sagging slightly and he was unable to fully close his right eye.

Immediately we brought him to our local doctor, who referred us to the children's unit at Tallaght Hospital. Aaron was then referred to a physiotherapist, Irene, who diagnosed him with a condition called Bell's palsy. She did exercises with him in an attempt to strengthen his facial muscles, but after many weeks of therapy there was no improvement. We were then referred to yet another doctor, Dr Webb. He performed a number of physical tests on Aaron, which included getting him to squeeze his fingers and close his eyes as tightly as he could. He also gently pushed him from side to side to test his balance. By the time he was sent for a CAT scan of his brain, we were very worried. Being only nine, Aaron didn't really understand the gravity of what was happening and, looking back, I suppose neither did we.

Barry had to work and wasn't able to be at the hospital the day these tests were being carried out. I clearly remember Dr Webb coming in to the room where I was waiting for the results with Aaron. He sat down beside me and asked if there was any way that I could get in touch with Barry to ask him to come to the hospital. My stomach hit the floor with the fright. I immediately rang Barry's base controller and asked him to give Barry the urgent message, and then sat for what seemed like an eternity waiting for him. When he eventually arrived, the doctor brought the two of us into a small room and had a nurse take Aaron to a different room to play with some toys. He began showing us the scan results. It's all a little blurry now, but I do remember struggling to concentrate on what he was saying. He informed us that he had discovered a growth on Aaron's brain stem and said he was going to send him to Beaumont Hospital, where they specialise in matters of the brain, for an MRI scan. They needed a more detailed picture of the growth before they knew exactly what they were dealing with.

After a couple of hours in Tallaght, we were taken by ambulance so that Aaron could be scanned and returned to Tallaght to await the results. We had so many questions we wanted answered. Was it a tumour? Was it cancer? Was it fixable and, above all, was our little man going to be OK? What the scan revealed was a large cyst wrapped around Aaron's brain stem. They suspected that he may have been born with it and as he grew, it grew. All his life-sustaining nerves were running through the growth and it was getting bigger. The weakness in his face was caused by the cyst stretching the nerve that works the facial muscles. Without this effect being so visually obvious, the cyst might have gone unnoticed until it was too late. The most worrying symptom was that, as it grew, it was stopping the flow of fluid around Aaron's brain, which meant that if it was not dealt with, it could lead to death.

Aaron spent a week in Tallaght hospital before being sent to Beaumont for brain surgery under the care of a neurosurgeon called Mr Alcutt. We were told that Aaron's condition was extremely rare; in fact, they said that they had never come across a case like it before. The day before the operation they sat us down and were brutally honest in telling us about the serious risks involved in the surgery. They explained that Aaron could develop epilepsy, or that he could end up being blind. They also said he could be paralysed in one or more parts of his body. Then, worst of all, there was the small but real chance that he wouldn't survive the operation. Our feelings of fear and helplessness were overwhelming.

The morning of the operation was horrendous. We tried to hold it together for Aaron, who was being so brave. On the walk down to theatre, I could hardly breathe and I prayed to my angels in heaven in desperation for them to come down and take care of him. When we reached the operating room, we were allowed to stay with him until he was asleep. Mr Alcutt asked Aaron if he had any requests, to which he replied, 'I don't want any stitches!' 'Of course,' the surgeon answered, and he promised to do his best. He was then asked by the anaesthetist to count down from ten but he only got to number five when his eyes closed. We both started to cry, as the emotional restraint for Aaron's sake fell away and we became the mess on the outside that we had been on the inside.

Surgery was expected to take between five and seven hours. We walked hand in hand like two zombies through the endless corridors of that hospital as we waited. The time seemed unending. When five hours had passed, we decided to wait in the corridor outside the operating room, because I couldn't wait anywhere else for fear of not being there when Aaron came out. Thankfully we weren't there too long before the theatre doors opened. The surgeon walked over to talk to us and said that the operation had gone very well, but that Aaron was still very heavily sedated and the full effect of the surgery was as yet unknown. He added that they were unsuccessful in removing the cyst but had managed to drain the fluid from the inside of it. He said that they also had to remove some of Aaron's skull to access the area and that they wouldn't be putting it back. This left us more than a little concerned, but the doctor reassured us that, in time, enough bone would grow, leaving only a small opening. Aaron was closely monitored over the next few hours and I became even more anxious, if that was possible. I just wanted a sign that under all the bandages, tubes and wires, my little boy was OK. At last he began to groan and made some small movements. It wasn't an indication of anything definite but at a time like this you hold on to even the smallest of things and we took great solace from it. Eventually that terrifying night got the better of me and I had to leave him for a few hours in the capable hands of Barry and the amazing nurses for some badly needed rest.

Over the following forty-eight hours Aaron began to wake up. To our huge relief he could see us, hear us and move all his limbs. Our worst fears had not happened. His recovery was slow, but after only two weeks we were allowed to take him home to recuperate. I wanted to buy the biggest roll of cotton wool to wrap him up in! The hospital had become our safe place where nothing could harm him, but I also realised that there is nowhere like your own home and bed to help speed up recovery. Besides, he was now our superhero and had many loved ones wanting to see him. After several months he was thankfully back to himself again, with the exception of his little face, which never fully recovered – though his smile was as beautiful as ever, and all the more welcome after everything he had been through.

3

Now that Aaron was well and back at school, I returned once again to my cleaning job with my sidekick Sinead. Our work varied from day to day, but we had one regular customer every fortnight, Bernadette Forde. She was the human resources manager at Guinness' brewery, and she lived in a beautifully decorated two-bedroom apartment in Donnybrook. Everything she owned, down to her cups and plates, was black or white: black blinds, white couches, white walls, black door frames. Even most of her hundreds of ornaments were one or the other, a few being glass or mirror. Bernadette had exquisite taste. We had a key to her apartment because she was at work most days. I was always terribly nervous while cleaning her things because I have been called a bit of a bull in a china shop. Mai used to call me 'Rough House Rosie' for that very reason.

Over the following few months Bernadette would often be home when we called. She was twelve years older than me. With shoulder-length dark blonde hair, she was quite full-figured and her face resembled the actress Meryl Streep, except Bernadette was prettier. I liked her from the very first time we met. She had the softest voice, with a mild Sligo accent and a gentle nature impossible to not warm to. We gelled so naturally and she seemed to like me too. We visited her every two weeks for the next several months until we got the news that the cleaning company we worked for was closing down. Sinead and I decided to go out on our own, so we contacted our regular customers, including Bernadette, and asked if they would like to keep the service going. Thankfully most of them did.

I began to notice that Bernadette was becoming slightly unstable on her feet, but in those early years I didn't know why. She was quite a private person and obviously didn't feel the need to explain. As sweet and lovely as she was, Bernadette had very exacting standards – something I was well used to since, growing up, my own mother had been the same in that regard. I later learned that being good at organising and arranging was vital for a human resources manager and it was a trait that was also evident in Bernadette's home: a place for everything and everything in its place. I often joked that she was like the character played by Kathy Bates in the movie *Misery* – if something was even slightly out of place, it was noticed almost immediately. I would also say I had something of an advantage over most people when I was around her. My mother was a very fussy woman, so I was programmed from an early age to handle this type of characteristic in someone.

Over time Bernadette explained what her illness was. She had primary progressive multiple sclerosis. It was my first time ever to hear of the disease. Soon after she told me, she had to retire from her job on medical grounds, which broke her heart because she loved working at Guinness. She had a great circle of friends there, all of whom she would greatly miss, and although it was possible that they might wish to visit her, Bernadette wasn't a big fan of people calling.

As time passed, although I still worked for Bernadette, our relationship developed into a friendship and I learned more about her and her past. She was born in Edgeworthstown in County Longford in 1959, the youngest of four girls. The nearest to her in age was Catherine, who was eleven years older, then came Beatrice and Marcena, the eldest. They had a brother, but he had died at a very young age. Her father was a railway stationmaster and her mother stayed at home to raise the children. Bernadette idolised her dad and always became terribly upset when speaking about him. I'm not too sure how old Bernadette was when he died but the wound of losing him never healed. She was his accidental baby girl and he doted on her. She loved her mother but explained to me that she was stern and harsh, often sending her out to the field to cut the very branch she was to be punished with. Apparently, Bernadette was a very big baby at birth, which caused irreparable injuries to her mother, with lifelong consequences. She felt her mother never forgave her, even though it was not her fault.

Bernadette attended college in Dublin and thrived in city life. Country living was just not exciting enough for her and when she moved to the capital, she never returned to Sligo – where they had moved to some years before. She always said the best part of travelling home to see her family in the country was returning to Dublin, that seeing the city lights ahead made her feel more at home than she did anywhere else.

Towards the end of 2005 Sinead informed me that she had secured a new job in a rehabilitation clinic, and so would not be continuing as a cleaner. I was gutted. I had such fun working alongside her and I was going to miss seeing her, but I understood her need for a more secure, full-time job. I contacted our regular customers and asked if they would like me to continue cleaning on my own. They all said yes.

Another year passed and now Bernadette was always home when I called. Of late there was a significant decline in her ability to walk with any stability. Her gait was increasingly wobbly, and it was beginning to affect her confidence. She insisted that I sit and chat with her instead of just cleaning. I would call into the Insomnia café before going to her apartment and buy a coffee for her and a hot chocolate for myself. We would then sip on them while we talked. I loved our conversations. I found Bernadette very interesting and she loved to hear all about my family. She had an enormous soft spot for Aaron, even though she had only met him a couple of times; in her eyes he could do no wrong no matter how much I complained about my hormone-filled growing boy. She would tilt her head and whisper, 'Ah but, Gail, he's only a baby!' She knew he had been through the mill with his health and so she made allowances off the back of it.

Although our age-gap was only twelve years, it always seemed much more. Bernadette had done so much in her life, and had experiences that I as a young mother never had, which made me think she was wiser and worldlier than me. She was a great advice-giver, and on countless occasions was a great support when I needed a shoulder to cry on. Over time what began as an employee/employer relationship grew to be a very close and loving friendship. I was aware that there was an openness between us which she didn't really show to others.

Over time Bernadette asked me if I could call a little more often, so I visited two, sometimes three, times a week. Along with the cleaning I began to do more varied jobs, such as gardening, painting and general DIY. There were many days when she would sit on her bed while I organised her entire and vast wardrobe. One of her many quirks was that everything in her wardrobe, along with her shoes, bags and jewellery, matched. She wouldn't be seen in public in anything less than perfect outfits. Although the jobs varied, the one thing I cherished was the fun we always had when we were together. There was now a lot of laughter in her home.

It was during one of our many talks that the subject of Dignitas came up. It is an organisation in Zurich, Switzerland, where one can go to avail of an assisted death. I had never heard of such a place. Bernadette, on the other hand, knew a lot about it and had clearly done much research on the subject. When informing me that she would one day be availing of their services, she was so practical, very matter-of-fact, as if it was nothing out of the ordinary. She knew the route she would take when her illness became too much for her to bear and I respected and understood her decision because it was in line with the black-and-white way her mind worked.

Every day I looked forward to seeing her, and she was now very comfortable having my support and the reassurance that someone was there to help her overcome the many – and increasing number of – obstacles of living with multiple sclerosis. She was also growing more unsteady on her legs and was having falls at home. In addition, she couldn't risk being out and about by herself, so I began keeping her company when she ventured out, including occasionally having lunch with her.

Early in 2007 Barry and I decided to change our jobs and become taxi drivers. Barry had a great geographical knowledge of Dublin from his days as a courier, but the poor man had to spend endless hours tutoring me. Without his constant teaching, I wouldn't have stood a chance of passing the test to become a taxi driver. When the day arrived to sit the SPSV test, we both passed with flying colours. We were thrilled.

This all happened when the Celtic Tiger was very much still alive, so we were in a position to borrow enough from our bank to buy two cars and our licences. Barry started working as a taxi driver in April 2007 and I followed in June. Even though I gave up cleaning to taxi full-time, I continued to visit Bernadette several times a week, still doing a variety of jobs around her home. At this stage she had become much more dependent on me and when she'd learned of my new job, she'd become terribly panicked and upset, thinking I wouldn't be calling any more. She was now so used to having my help that we agreed between us that I would continue to call as often as she wanted me to.

4

On the morning of 11 February 2008 I called over to Bernadette. We had made an arrangement to go out to lunch together. For a change, I put on a girlie outfit for the day. My usual attire would be more tomboyish – jeans, a T-shirt and hiking boots – but Bernadette liked it when I dressed up a little more when we went out. Lunch this day was her treat. She was bringing me to the restaurant in the Brown Thomas store on Grafton Street. I had never been to Brown Thomas; it was a little posher than I was used to but was one of Bernadette's favourite places to shop.

At this time, Bernadette was still well enough to drive her own car. She drove a Toyota Yaris and, although it was automatic and modified with hand controls, her stubbornness and determination to maintain her independence meant that she continued to use the foot pedals. I would be lying if I said I wasn't a little nervous as a passenger. We headed off from her apartment in Donnybrook at around noon. It was quite a jumpy journey but I wasn't going to be the one to pull the rug from under Bernadette by telling her that she should not be driving. Besides, she wouldn't have listened to me.

We drove through Dublin, randomly chatting about this and that, putting the world to rights as we often did. We entered the Brown Thomas indoor car park at about 12.30 p.m., still yapping away and giggling like two schoolchildren. As we drove in we passed by two men standing beside a silver convertible car. In high spirits, Bernadette said something humorous to them through her open window about men's mid-life crises and they smiled back. Then we went down the small incline where Bernadette took a ticket and went through the barrier. Everything still seemed fine, but as we moved forward and veered right, something went terribly wrong.

It all happened so quickly that there was very little time to react. Bernadette suddenly slumped forward, with almost her entire body weight on the steering wheel. She struggled to control the car but couldn't. We picked up speed at an alarming rate because her leg had gone into a spasm and was pressing down on the accelerator. I clearly remember the whooshing sound as we passed the cars parked to our left, and screamed Bernadette's name at the top of my voice. She didn't respond.

In front of us at the other end of the car park was a concrete wall and we were heading straight for it. The car continued to speed up. Somehow I managed to grab hold of the shoulder part of my seatbelt and was able to pull my legs towards my chest just before the car ploughed into the wall. I felt as if I'd been hit by a train. Within seconds of the impact, the inside of the car filled with smoke. I couldn't catch my breath because of the excruciating pain in my chest, and felt extremely disoriented. I thought the car was on fire and frantically searched for the door handle. I couldn't see anything, not even Bernadette. Eventually I opened my door and fell out onto the ground. I'm sure I would have screamed more but I wasn't able to fill my lungs with enough air. I really thought I was dying.

I became aware that there were people around us, shouting. I kept repeating, 'Is Bernadette OK?' The next thing I knew, a woman was kneeling over me. If my memory serves me correctly, she told me her name was Amy. She placed her knees on either side of my head in an attempt to stop me from moving, but I begged her to check on Bernadette. However, she refused to leave my side. She tried to reassure me, saying that others were attending to my friend. There was so much commotion. I could hear a baby crying and someone roaring, 'Call an ambulance! Call an ambulance!'

It felt like a very long time before the ambulances arrived and I still had no information about how badly Bernadette was injured. My breathing seemed to be getting worse; I was struggling to catch even a small breath at this stage. I was also now aware of severe pain in other parts of my body. The paramedics hurriedly but gently placed me on a stretcher and put me into the back of one of the ambulances. I managed to look over and saw about six or seven people huddled around the driver's side of the car where Bernadette still was. I feared the worst because no one was telling me anything.

I was taken to St James' Hospital and brought straight to Accident and Emergency. As fuzzy as my memories are, I recall the pain and I also remember calling for Barry over and over. Eventually he arrived, as did the morphine, bringing its wonderful numbness to my very sore and broken body. There was still no news of Bernadette. I was sent for X-rays, CT scans and various other tests. These revealed that I had torn my bowel, and it was causing internal bleeding. I also had a fractured collarbone, deep cuts to my legs and chest and severely torn ligaments in my right ankle. My heart had also been damaged in the impact: it had been crushed between my chest bone and spine by the seatbelt, causing a distressing irregular heart rhythm. Two less serious conditions that resulted from the accident were tinnitus and vertigo.

I spent that first anxious and restless night in the cardiac observation room. The surgery to repair my torn bowel was scheduled for the following morning. At this stage the only information Barry and I had about Bernadette was that she was alive but in a coma. Bernadette's sister Catherine, who was closest in age to her out of her three older sisters, came in to see me. She was accompanied by her son-in-law, Shane. It was the first time for Catherine and I to meet. She was visibly distressed and worried sick about Bernadette. Catherine was slim, with shoulder-length brown hair, very friendly and soft-spoken. She filled me in about Bernadette's injuries. She said that as a result of Bernadette's right leg being stuck straight out when the car hit the wall, her legs had taken most of the impact. They were very badly damaged and trapped in the wreckage, and the rescue services had to cut her from the car. She had also seriously injured her liver and required urgent surgery. Catherine told me that Bernadette would be transferred to St Vincent's hospital, which specialises in liver procedures. She would be brought back to St James' afterwards. I was so grateful to Catherine for coming in with news about my friend. It wasn't good news but it was better than where my tormented imaginings had been taking me.

The following morning came and went, as did my surgery, which took about three hours. Thankfully it was a success. I slept for most of the afternoon and had a few visitors throughout the late afternoon and early evening. I still had only limited information about Bernadette. The worry weighed heavily on me. The following day when Barry arrived, I told him I wanted to visit Bernadette in the intensive care unit. Because I was still too weak and in too much pain to walk far, he asked a nurse if we could borrow one of the wheelchairs from the ward. She agreed.

As I was wheeled through the corridors, I felt a mixture of nerves and dread at the thought of seeing Bernadette. At the ICU Barry pressed the buzzer and we were shown in by one of the nurses. At the entrance we had to dress from top to toe in sterile gowns. It was my first time in an intensive care ward and it all felt surreal. There were five or six beds and the nurse showed us to Bernadette's. As long as I live, I will never forget seeing her there. She was almost unrecognisable, and there were all kinds of wires and tubes coming from her battered body. She was bloated to almost double her normal size and her tongue was hanging out one side of her mouth. I burst into tears. How in God's name had a simple outing to lunch turned into such a nightmare?

Barry pushed my chair alongside Bernadette's bed, and all I could do was sit there and cry. Barry himself was visibly shaken. I did my best to compose myself and began talking to Bernadette. I wasn't sure if she was aware that we were there, but I hoped so much that she could hear my voice. There was no reaction. We left after about an hour, and I sobbed all the way back to my ward. The following day Barry and I made our way back again to intensive care but when we pressed the buzzer, instead of allowing us to enter, the nurse came out. She asked me my name and then went back inside. When she returned, she told me that I wouldn't be allowed to go in. When I asked why, she told me that one of Bernadette's sisters had left specific instructions that I was not to be allowed in to pay a visit.

What the hell was going on? I was very upset because I had no idea why such a decision had been made. I'd had only the one visit from Catherine, so information about Bernadette remained limited. A friend of Bernadette's, Mary Lundy, dropped in to see me once or twice, so I figured she might be my best bet to find out what was going on. Mary and Bernadette had been friends for almost twenty-five years. They had once worked together as civil servants, and had remained close ever since. I had got to know Mary when I'd cleaned her house once or twice in the past. I asked her if she had any idea why Bernadette's family would stop me from visiting her. She had no answer.

I felt so helpless, and couldn't get my head around the fact that I wasn't allowed to visit my sick friend. It almost killed me that I had absolutely no control over the situation. It was as if, to her family, I was a nobody. One day Barry and I bumped into two of the sisters, Beatrice and Marcena, in the hospital canteen but the meeting was very strained as they did little to hide their discomfort around me. What had I done to cause this animosity?

A week later I was released from hospital. I couldn't wait to get home, back to my comfortable bed and familiar surroundings, but my heart was breaking at leaving Bernadette behind, not knowing if or when I would see her again. I knew from Mary that she was still in a coma but that her liver surgery had been successful. I longed to see her.

Days turned into weeks and I still had no contact with the family. Bernadette remained in a coma and there was very little improvement in her condition.

By May 2008 I myself was well on the road to recovery but still attending various doctors about my heart condition: I suffered from a frequent skipped heartbeat. It was occurring about thirty times every minute and was growing increasingly distressing.

I was also receiving regular physiotherapy treatments. I knew one of the biggest things that would help me recover was to return to work, and it took a lot of gentle coaxing, and even a little arguing from Barry before I eventually agreed to get back behind the wheel of the cab. Not only did I have to overcome so many fears and emotions, I also had to regain enough confidence to drive others around in my taxi.

I was at home one afternoon when my phone rang. It was Bernadette calling from the hospital! I couldn't believe it. I was so overwhelmed with relief that I started sobbing. We only talked for a short while because she didn't have much energy, but we made arrangements for me to come to see her in St James'. I was so happy to hear from her, but I was nervous on my way to the hospital as I didn't know what the reception would be like if any of her family were visiting at the same time. Thankfully, Bernadette was alone when I arrived. I was taken aback by her appearance – rather than being bloated, as she was when I last saw her, she had by now lost a lot of weight and looked quite unwell. Her ordeal over the last three months showed in her gaunt frame. Our reunion was emotional, to say the least, but we were overjoyed to see each other again. We hugged and cried and talked about the craziness of the crash. She told me that it had taken three operations to set her liver to rights. Her legs were a mess and would need to use a wheelchair for the foreseeable future. Her knees were screwed and pinned together, and they had had to put metal rods in her legs to support her shattered bones. Her once-porcelain skin now had many scars, which deeply upset her. She told me the scar she hated the most was the one on her throat from the tracheotomy tube. I mentioned that I had not been allowed in to see her, but she didn't have the energy to discuss it. I dropped the subject for fear of upsetting her. Over the following weeks I visited Bernadette regularly.

Although she couldn't walk, her general health improved and she was getting stronger. Late in July, the doctors at St James' explained to Bernadette that there was little more they could do for her, so they were going to transfer her to Clontarf orthopaedic hospital on the northside of Dublin. The hospital specialises in that 'next' step of recovery from injuries. Bernadette was anxious about leaving the familiar surroundings and staff of St James', but she knew it was the right thing to do.

At Clontarf she had a lovely room all to herself. The place was a lot less clinical than St James', which greatly helped her recovery. I continued to visit a few times a week. Bernadette was definitely happier there but was still extremely homesick. About four weeks after her transfer, she and I were chatting about her progress. She was slowly getting used to being in a wheelchair. In saying that, she hated it with every fibre of her being, but she relied on it so much for her limited freedom that she had no choice but to get on with it. She was also receiving regular, intensive physiotherapy and her general attitude was positive. I was pleased for her that she now had a degree of hope for the future, along with a lot of determination to keep going. It was during one of our many chats that I suggested asking one of the nurses if I could take Bernadette out. The only world she had seen for months was the inside of various wards or the small patch of grass in the grounds of the hospital where we would often sit if the weather was warm enough, so we set about finding someone to ask. When we did find a nurse, she hemmed and hawed a little but finally said yes.

I would be lying if I said that we weren't both a little nervous. The last time we had been in a car together hadn't turned out too well, and now I was in charge of a very delicate, sickly, wheelchair-bound person. Still, it didn't matter because she was Thelma and I was Louise and we were going on an adventure. Before we could go anywhere, though, I had the unenviable task of trying to figure out how Bernadette's wheelchair worked. Eventually I got the foot supports off and the armrest up and positioned her alongside my car. She carefully shimmied her way on to the passenger seat. I could see the pain on her face as I gently lifted her legs into the footwell. Hooray, she was in! Then fifteen more minutes were spent trying to fold the wheelchair while she laughed at my efforts.

On that first nerve-wracking outing, we didn't venture too far. We first headed back to St James' to buy Bernadette the grapefruit juice she had become addicted to while staying there. I used to buy all that was on the shelf in the shop and she would keep the containers in a cooler box beside her bed. We then drove back towards Clontarf and stopped for lunch in Clontarf Castle. It was a very big deal for Bernadette to be seen out in public in a wheelchair. Before the crash, she needed only the aid of a walking stick and, although she had bought one or two beautiful canes, even these were an embarrassment to her.

Once in the restaurant, she transferred to a dining chair. It was so wonderful to be out together! We were both in flying form. I dropped her back to the hospital a couple of hours later, getting her safely to her room. That day was a good day and these had been few and far between for her of late. This new-found freedom definitely helped Bernadette's mental well-being. She realised that her world hadn't ended because she had ventured out in public in a wheelchair. She had done it and so had conquered a huge fear. From that point on, her confidence grew. Weeks passed, bringing many more outings. We would be gone for hours.

We went to Blackrock, St Stephen's Green, Liffey Valley – it really didn't matter where, just that we were getting out again. I went from being a nervous minder to taking on the world for my friend. It was so good to see the old Bernadette come back to life.

Always at the back of her mind she knew that someday even Clontarf would have nothing more to offer her. For many, a temporary stay in a nursing or convalescent home would be the next option, but not for Bernadette. One of her greatest fears was staying in a nursing home, but her choices of where to live were limited. Catherine, who ran a bed and breakfast in her own house just outside Roscommon town, asked her to come and stay with her. She had lots of en suite rooms, but Bernadette, while grateful for the offer, refused to live in the countryside.

I was sitting at home with Barry one evening talking about Bernadette's predicament when he came up with a great solution. He suggested that I become a carer or an aid to Bernadette, if she was agreeable to the idea. I was delighted with his suggestion. I was already seeing her regularly, but mostly fitting around my schedule. So I texted Bernadette with this offer, which could possibly help her overcome the many obstacles she would have to face in the near future. Her grateful and emotional response was also filled with both relief and excitement. She was over the moon, and we set about making plans.

Her apartment was small and narrow and totally unsuitable for a wheelchair user. Simply getting in and out of her front door, with its high step and tiny hallway, was going to be an ordeal, but I knew if we put our heads together we could solve most of the problems. She would also have to buy herself a wheelchair to replace the one belonging to the hospital. So first things first! We went to see a lovely man called Paddy in the Irish Wheelchair Association and he arranged everything for Bernadette. She bought comfy cushions and a slider board to make it easier when transferring from the chair to the loo and other tricky places.

Bernadette's last day in Clontarf was a mixture of fear and happiness. She feared leaving the security of the hospital but was also bursting to get home. We pulled up outside her door filled with anxiety. Once the car was emptied and Bernadette was safely indoors, I began moving around furniture. She delegated and I carried out her requests. One major obstacle was her bathroom. The door was unusually narrow and her wheelchair wouldn't fit through it. This problem was solved when I bridged the gap from her loo to the door with her dining chairs. I taped the chair legs together so they wouldn't move and she was able to shimmy across them. Day by day, piece by piece, her apartment became both safer and more accessible.

Over the following weeks I was with Bernadette

almost every day. There was so much to be done. She remained a little tense, but with time got her head around her new way of life. Her confidence continued to grow, as did her determination. When we were together, even the most difficult obstacles were overcome with fun and humour; sometimes they are the best tonic for getting through a tough day. She was in a considerable amount of pain all the time, but she bore it with grace. Her poor legs caused her the most upset. She was unable to lie down because the pain intensified when she did, so she slept in her wheelchair most of the time.

We still went out quite a lot, mostly shopping, always one of Bernadette's favourite pastimes. She needed to replace most of her wardrobe because she had dropped from a size 26 to a 12, and her clothes no longer fitted her. We would sit for hours in various cafés just watching the world go by. For the time being, she accepted that the wheelchair was a necessary evil but she also truly believed that one day she would walk again. It's funny, but it is only when you are in a position of caring for someone with a disability or indeed are disabled yourself that you realise how inconsiderate the human race can be in relation to respecting either disabled toilets or parking spaces. I lost count of the number of times we were forced to confront one of these people. When visiting the Jervis Shopping Centre in Dublin, I always struggled to find an available, convenient disabled parking space.

It got to the point where I was forced to approach the management of the car park because I noticed that a lot of the cars using these spaces didn't have a permit displayed. The manager informed me that an able-bodied young woman who worked in the centre used one of the disabled spaces. Apparently she had been asked on a number of occasions not to park there but she had chosen to ignore the requests. So I did what any caring friend would do. I let the air out of a couple of her tyres while Bernadette watched, giggling. Then I placed a little note on the windscreen, which read, 'You're disabled now!' She never parked there again.

Days turned into weeks and slowly Bernadette became strong and confident enough to spend some days at home alone. Regaining a modicum of independence was something she greatly valued. There were still many hospital appointments for her to keep and she also attended regular physiotherapy in St James' Hospital. Doing her exercises was a painful struggle but she longed to walk again, so she did her very best. It was difficult for me to watch her while she struggled on the parallel bars, grimacing in pain. Often it was just too much for her, resulting in many tears being shed. The physiotherapy sessions continued at home, and we would do the exercises together daily. Her occupational therapist, Helen Lee, provided her with a Zimmer frame in the hope that it would help. I would follow closely behind with her wheelchair to catch her when she fell but her efforts were too risky and short-lived. As time went by she became increasingly agitated but she refused to admit defeat. Crutches were also bought but, sadly, tried only once or twice before they too were tossed angrily to one side. One day was particularly upsetting and she was inconsolable, saying that she wished the car crash had ended her life.

Bernadette strongly believed in mind over matter, so she booked herself in for a ten-week course of hypnotherapy at the famous Paul Golden clinic in Dun Laoghaire. She was under the care of a lovely woman called Mary. The sessions consisted of hypnosis and meditative relaxation. It was a lovely place, with truly wonderful intentions, but no amount of positive thinking could undo the physical damage to her legs. Bernadette was hugely disappointed at the end of the course that, in spite of giving it her best shot, none of the methods ultimately worked.

5

Bernadette's multiple sclerosis was getting much worse. The constant painful spasms in her legs caused her great discomfort and anguish. Her disease was stifling any attempts to walk again and the distress of this seemed to accelerate her illness. She was giving up the fight a little more with each passing day and I saw her will to thrive begin to fade. It was over these torturous weeks that the subject of Dignitas made its way more regularly into our conversations. Again, she always brought it up in her usual matter-of-fact way but she was focused on it now more than ever.

In July 2010 her sister Marcena was losing her own battle with sickness. She had suffered from cancer on and off for years, always overcoming the odds, but this time, sadly, the cancer was winning. Bernadette and I travelled a couple of times to Sligo so she could spend time with her family, and we were there in the days running up to Marcena's death. Bernadette refused to stay in the house at night, so we booked in to the Glasshouse Hotel in the centre of the town. Our days were spent with Bernadette's family but at night she loved nothing more than getting into her comfortable night clothes and ordering from room service a couple of her favourite drinks, Bombay Sapphire gin martinis. The days were long and exhausting for her. On top of that, Marcena's house wasn't modified in any way for a wheelchair user and, although there was a stair lift, it was torture for Bernadette trying to navigate getting on and off it.

Bernadette's nephew Bernard was amazing in those last days of his Aunt Marcena's life. He nursed her around the clock, which was heartbreaking for him. From what I have gathered, they were always very close. Witnessing what had to be done on a personal basis for her sister had a profound effect on Bernadette. She spoke often about her greatest fear, which was being nursed, wiped and washed by someone, something that would be avoided if she chose to travel to Switzerland. Watching Bernard, as amazing as he was, definitely made her think of her own demise, which in her eyes was rapidly approaching.

A day or two later Marcena slipped away very peacefully. We were all assembled around the house in different rooms, not really knowing what to do. Bernadette took me quietly to one side and asked me to gather certain members of her family together because she wanted to talk with them. She asked that I just inform Bernard, Catriona (Catherine's daughter) and Catherine of her wishes. I did as she asked and left the four of them in the living room to talk. I knew what she was about to announce. She didn't want her sister Beatrice present for the talk because she could predict her reaction. Her request for respect and understanding would not be met with anything but objections, so she opted not to tell her. Beatrice was very religious, a strict pro-life supporter, so the idea of her baby sister taking her own life, which Beatrice firmly believed was ultimately only God's to take, wasn't something she would accept, which would inevitably cause Bernadette more upset than she was already experiencing.

Some time later, Bernadette told me that she had informed her family of her intentions to use the services of Dignitas. She said that both Catriona and Catherine became upset at the news and questioned if it was the best thing. Bernard, however, unsurprisingly took it better. He is very practical, and I think Bernadette always knew that he would be supportive of her decision. I understood how such a conversation could be upsetting, but I also knew first-hand how hard Bernadette's life had become and the enormous difficulties she faced just getting through each twenty-four hours. Maybe her black-and-white attitude to it all had rubbed off on me over the many years of our friendship. Either way, she always had my understanding and support. She needed me to handle these matters in as uncomplicated a way as possible, causing her as little stress as I could.

Marcena's wake and funeral also helped Bernadette make decisions about her own laying to rest. The traditional Catholic ways did not appeal to her as they had to her sister, such as mirrors in the house being covered, and curtains being closed on the windows. Yet Bernadette was one of the most spiritual people I have ever met in her own way. She had a great faith in angels, God and an afterlife. She very much trusted that there was reincarnation, truly believing that she had passed this way more than once. When she was younger, she had undergone past-life regression and felt she had lived many lives, believing that a soul returns only to learn lessons and repair any hurt it has caused on its journeys. Mistakes made in previous lives had to be rectified in the next, and only when the soul was cleansed of all wrong-doing could it make its final journey to heaven, never needing to return.

Bernadette was devoted to the ideas outlined in Rhonda Byrne's best-selling book *The Secret*, that positive thinking and visualisation, being grateful for what you have, can create positive energy in the universe, and ultimately lead to a greater happiness. Being grateful not for riches or possessions, but the simple things we often take for granted in our busy lives, such as a roof over our head, food in our press or someone who loves us. I too now share these philosophies and do my best to pass them on to my close family and friends. There are many who see it all as gobbledegook, but for me it works, even if only inside my own head. It makes me happier and more aware of how lucky I am if I do my best to always remember the good fortune I have in abundance. Bernadette once bought me a gratitude journal so I could write down the things I am grateful for but there were too many to list; it now sits in a drawer in my bedroom alongside the many beautiful and heartfelt gifts she bought for me.

After Marcena's funeral, Bernadette and I stayed one more night in Sligo before heading back to Dublin. The lights of Dublin reflecting on the clouds guiding us home put a big smile on Bernadette's face. We stopped along the way for her favourite almond Magnum ice cream and her drug of choice, an americano coffee. She was happily back to her comfort zone.

Throughout all the years and months she and I spent together, we regularly went for lunch with her niece Catriona and her little girl Kate, whom Bernadette adored. She would often say that she liked children only between the ages of two and eight, before, in her opinion, they became annoying, but when it came to Kate those rules went out the window. She took so many photographs of her that she filled an entire wall in her bedroom with pictures of her, calling it 'the Kate wall'. The photographs were displayed in chronological order, fitting in with Bernadette's need for perfection and structure. She regularly sat for quite a long time just going from picture to picture, often reduced to tears because she loved Kate so much.

It was now late 2010 and her health was worse than ever; every day there was a significant deterioration in what she was able to do. Her pain and discomfort were taking a huge toll on her physical and mental well-being. She had modified her home as much as the small space available would allow. Internal doors were removed and doorways widened, kitchen counters were lowered in an attempt to keep her as independent as possible, but she still struggled more and more. My son Aaron built a concrete ramp leading up to her front door but she was now too weak to negotiate it. Days and nights were a living hell. She began having more and more falls from her wheelchair, mostly when transferring to the toilet. She often forgot to bring her phone into the bathroom with her and sometimes spent hours trying to drag her sore and broken body to the living room so she could ring me for help. She called Barry her 'picker upper' because he was the only one strong enough to pick her up and place her gently back in her chair. He dealt with these situations with the respect she required and would then wait outside in the car for as long as it took me to make Bernadette comfortable and feeling safe again. Sometimes it would be two or three hours before I was able to leave her because she was so distressed.

Bernadette now hated being alone at home. Eventually, after much persuasion, she bought an alarm which she wore around her neck. When she had a fall, she just pressed a button which contacted a controller. A comforting voice would come through speakers placed around her home and she could tell them what had happened. It was my number they had on record. I worried about her a little less, knowing she now had this system in place. Then there were the nights when she would simply drop something, usually the remote control for the television. She spent twenty-four hours a day stuck in her wheelchair. The only sleep she managed to get was an hour or two with her legs on the couch and her back to the roaring gas fire. Television was her sole companion when I wasn't there, so dropping the remote control and being unable to pick it up was very bad news. One day I created what we referred to as 'the sticky stick'. I wrapped gaffer tape, sticky side out, around the end of one of her now unused walking canes which was ideal for retrieving things from the floor. It worked a treat, and we were delighted with my simple but effective invention.

From around July of 2010 our outings together were becoming increasingly difficult. Bernadette's body was so very sore that she struggled to do the very things she had managed to do only weeks before. What little energy she had was fading. A couple of years previously she had bought an electric wheelchair, hoping it would make things easier. Unfortunately, owing to her poor reflexes and lack of strength, it resulted in one too many unnerving crashes into people and obstacles and she lost what little confidence she had. So it was parked up, covered over and never used again. Nothing now brought Bernadette any comfort, except Kate, who was her most beautiful distraction.

November arrived and it was time to begin organising her Christmas. It was one of her favourite seasons and she spoiled everyone she loved to a ridiculous extent. Our days were filled with endless trips to the various shopping centres around Dublin. She would choose and I would queue. When the handles of her wheelchair were too crammed with shopping bags, I would put them in my car before beginning to fill the handles again. Evenings were spent sitting on her living room floor sorting and wrapping all she had bought while we ate a curry from her local Chinese take-away. I loved these late evenings in her company, with her gas fire on full and winter blowing a gale outside. Bernadette's vast array of Christmas decorations matched her immaculate home furnishings, with tons of black, white, mirrored and crystal adornments of all shapes and sizes. It took us two full days to complete the job of decorating her home for Christmas.

Regretfully that Christmas marked our last outing together. It was December 2010, the year of the really big snow. One night we returned from shopping about ten o'clock. Driving conditions were treacherous and we were both very relieved to get back to her apartment in one piece. Because of the high snow drifts, I was unable to park in the usual spot outside her front door, instead having to do so about sixty feet away. It was such a struggle simply getting her from the car into her wheelchair, not helped by the driving snow and sub-zero temperatures. Our next hurdle was trying to push a rather heavy lady, with a lap piled so high with presents that she couldn't see over it, through the deep snow. I ended up having to drag her wheelchair backwards but the snow kept wedging itself underneath, so I had to keep stopping to dig it out with my hands. We both got the biggest fit of giggles. It took even longer because I was laughing so hard – it was making me weak – but eventually I got her to and through her front door, back into the warmth she loved so much.

As well as the laughter, however, there was also, increasingly, a sad and serious side to these events. It was clear to both of us how difficult everything had become; worse than ever, in fact. Even when out and about, Bernadette's difficulties using disabled toilets made doing so almost impossible. The upper body strength she greatly relied on was diminishing by the day, so transferring her to and from the loo was painful and extremely dangerous. There was also a significant reduction in her ability to control her bladder and bowels, resulting in frequent accidents at home and in public. She was really upset at this new problem. After much persuasion, she allowed me to buy pads recommended by her pharmacy, but this too was a nightmare for her. I would change them, but Bernadette's attempts to hold herself up off the chair long enough for me to replace the pad failed more often than not. She regularly broke down in tears of frustration and anger. Her worst fear was losing her independence and dignity, and these realities were now knocking loudly on her door. She was very frightened a lot of the time as her MS crept at an alarming rate across her entire body.

Within a couple of days of that particularly difficult shopping trip, Bernadette brought up the subject of Dignitas again, but this time she was more sure and decisive in her tone. If I'm honest, it didn't shock or surprise me. I knew that one day it would become a reality. She had mentioned it so often throughout the years that the subject no longer alarmed me. Even the phraseology she used, which to others would be so shocking, rolled off me like the proverbial water off a duck's back. She often quipped that she simply wanted them to 'put me down and post me home'. Initially, I was shocked at this bluntness but she just laughed at my reaction and carried on as normal. The route to end her life made utter sense to her. No mess, no fuss, just black and white.

Over the following few days she asked that I get a contact phone number and email address for Dignitas. She also asked me to make the first call to their office in Zurich. I spoke to a lovely young man called Silvan, who explained all about the service they provide, and what first steps Bernadette needed to take. He explained what paperwork he would be sending her and what to do with it. They don't simply say yes to you; there is a lot to be done before you even reach that stage. He was extremely compassionate, which made making that call a lot easier. Bernadette became very focused on the job at hand and began instructing me to write list upon list of things she required.

Dignitas asks for affidavits, medical records dating back ten years, a birth certificate, letters of compos mentis to confirm that she was in her right mind, the list was long. Bernadette was now house-bound, so it was my job to source all these things for her. My days were spent queuing in various government departments. The affidavit was to ensure that Bernadette had never married nor had any children. Medical reports would confirm her illness and its progression. The letters of compos mentis from a doctor were to confirm that she was of sound mind and body and capable of making decisions, including those related to Dignitas. It took a couple of weeks to gather the necessary documentation. Only on one occasion was Bernadette required to visit a solicitor, so she hired a van from a company called Vantastic which brought her to an office in Drimnagh. Respectfully the solicitor came and sat in the van with her, saving her from the stress of having to get out.

Gradually, the items on Bernadette's many lists were ticked off, much to her great relief. Personally, my stress levels were increasing but I never let her know; instead I offloaded on Barry when I returned home in the evenings. Bernadette was being so strong, the last thing she needed was the weight of my emotions burdening her. Barry was my sanctuary, the one who saw me break down and cry and, although I fully supported Bernadette's decisions, the situation was beginning to take its toll on me. Without Barry I would have caved in under the sadness of it all.

I was now spending every day with Bernadette. She was so unwell and struggling with so much that she needed someone to be there seven days a week. She was exhausted all the time and not getting any break from the constant pain. She bought a commode in an attempt to remain somewhat independent, but after only a week or two it was put in her spare room alongside all the other aids that no longer met her needs. Losing this last vestige of her dignity almost pushed her over the edge emotionally. She wanted to escape her crippling illness long before she reached this stage, but regretfully her weakening body had different ideas and this once independent woman had no choice but to deal pragmatically with what was happening to her. As always, together we overcame any awkwardness or embarrassment, mostly through inappropriate humour and laughter. Seeing the 'funny' in difficult situations is sometimes all you can do to get through them, and that we managed in abundance.

All the while the cogs of her Dignitas plans continued to turn. She had sent them the paperwork they had requested and now she waited for what they refer to as the 'provisional green light', a term they use when they have accepted you as one of their clients. It means that you are free to avail of their services at any time of your choosing. Ironically, eighty-five per cent of the people who receive the provisional green light never end their life in Dignitas. They seem to settle into whatever illness they are suffering from and get on with living. It's having the comfort of an option that is important, a back-up plan should things become unbearable.

Bernadette received her green light about two weeks after she had sent in the application. It was an enormous weight lifted from her. Her new focus was on emptying her apartment. She wanted to return gifts and trinkets that had been given to her from family and friends. She, Catherine and I boxed up most of her possessions, which Catherine and her husband Brian brought to their home in Roscommon to be stored. Bernadette had a new-found energy while doing all this. She was enjoying being in control of her life. She hadn't yet set a date to travel to Zurich, but it was clear that it would be sooner rather than later.

Catherine was dealing with the sorrow and pain as best she could. Like myself, she had spoken to Bernadette about the possibility of being cared for in the final stages of her life in a care home, but Bernadette was adamantly against this. She asked me once why on earth Bernadette wanted to die in a foreign country surrounded by strangers. But I knew why Bernadette would not consider ending her life with dignity at home. She feared greatly that she would be unsuccessful in her attempt and, when found, the authorities would commit her. She also didn't want the stress of having her loved ones around when it all happened. She was sure she would feel in safe hands with the professionals in Dignitas.

Roughly two weeks after she received the green light, Bernadette decided on a date to travel. She felt ready. Her home was almost empty apart from the day-to-day things she required, and her finances were in order, with all outstanding bills taken care of. A huge worry, and a reason for her making the date, was that her swallow was beginning to weaken and she often choked when eating or drinking, so she was concerned that if she left it any longer, she wouldn't be able to drink the lethal dose in Dignitas, which is the only method they use. You must drink it yourself with no help from the staff.

Next to be decided was who was going to travel to Zurich with her. I would accompany her, but we needed help because there was a lot to carry. Catherine wanted to come but, owing to an illness, was unable to fly. Bernadette decided to ask her nephew Bernard to come with us. He accepted without hesitation. As I have already mentioned, he is a wonderful man who could be relied on to handle the stress with great assurance. He was always very supportive of his aunt's decision.

Bernadette chose to use a travel agent in Rathgar village to book the journey. Initial arrangements were made over the phone and I called once to the travel agent's to go through the details. Because Bernadette was committing a legal act in a country where assisted suicide was legal, she felt no reason to withhold information. In fact she insisted on total honesty, telling the travel agent the reason for the trip. I booked three flights to Zurich travelling on 26 April 2011, with two of us returning three days later. So far all seemed to be going according to plan. The last thing the travel agent said to me was that they would be in touch to arrange a date and time for me to collect the tickets. I received that call a couple of days later, and was told that the tickets would be ready for collection on Wednesday, 20 April. Bernadette was comforted in the knowledge that her plans were coming together.

6

Wednesday, 20 April 2011 began the same as almost every other day. I arrived at Bernadette's apartment at around 11 a.m. She was sitting as usual in her wheelchair in the living room, watching telly beside the roaring gas fire. Most days the heat from the fire was unbearable, but Bernadette always felt cold, so it remained on, no matter what the season. On my way to her apartment, I had picked up coffee for Bernadette and a hot chocolate for myself and now we sat, sipping them, while making plans for the day ahead. There was still so much organising and running around to be done for our trip.

Bernadette had spent so many weeks sorting out her belongings that her home was almost empty. She had also closed bank and credit union accounts and paid the balance on outstanding bills. The large Jiffy bags we had bought earlier in the week were filled with trinkets and cards for friends. These had been little gifts Bernadette had received throughout the years which she wanted to return. At the moment she was happily focused on ticking off all the things on her 'to do' list. By nature Bernadette was an extremely organised person, and derived great pleasure and peace of mind from the fact that she was still in control of her own affairs. I sat, as I always did, facing her, writing out a long list of instructions from her: people to phone, businesses to contact, arranging the Swiss currency for our trip, and so on.

A couple of days earlier Bernadette and I had sat for hours, sorting through her old photographs. While doing so, we reminisced about better days gone by. She became quite upset; never had she imagined life turning out this way. Some of these photos were included in her return gifts. One very important thing she wanted to leave behind was a big brown folder on which were written the words 'For the gardaí'. It was full of important paperwork that included copies of letters to and from Dignitas, correspondence about her illness, and other letters confirming her mental well-being from two doctors. She had also hand-written two letters that gave details about our relationship, and the role I played in her life. She was leaving this folder behind for the authorities in case there were any questions about her intentions. She wanted to make it clear that everything that was done was her decision, and that it was understood that taking her life was her choice and hers alone. Another thing she wanted to do was to write a 'suicide note'. The problem was that her hands were getting weaker every day, and she knew her note would more than likely end up being a lengthy letter. At the time I was doing any writing she needed, but there was no way I could have written such a note.

Bernadette, always resourceful, decided to buy a Dictaphone. She called an electrical shop, Peats of Parnell Street, and ordered one. It was delivered two days later. When it arrived, she asked me to sit and write down her spoken words. When finished, she read what I had written and then spoke the words into the Dictaphone. I realise this may all seem quite surreal, but when you are absorbed into such a situation, it was just another practical item that needed to be done. When Bernadette had finished speaking into the machine, we played the tape back to ensure that she was happy with it. She then asked me to call Barry and play it down the phone to him.

I knew he would be shocked to hear her request, but I also knew he would oblige. After we played it, it was apparent that it was upsetting for him to listen to, because I could hear a faint tremble in his tone when he responded. He confirmed that it covered all the information Bernadette wanted the authorities to know. When it came to items that were to be given back to her family, she drummed it into my head who was to get what because the last thing she wanted was for there to be any disharmony. She thought it was best to have specific, detailed instructions.

Bernadette still hadn't told her sister Beatrice of her plans to end her life abroad. Several people, including Catherine and her family, knew, and Beatrice's own son Bernard not only knew but intended to travel to Switzerland with us. When I asked Bernadette when she was going to tell Beatrice, she brushed me off. Then she said, 'I'll ring her from Zurich and tell her then.' This then changed to, 'I'm not telling her at all!' I was more than a little concerned.

I tried my best to talk to Bernadette about this. I explained how hurt Beatrice would be, regardless of the trouble Bernard could find himself in with his mother upon his return from Zurich. But she was having none of it. Deep down she knew Beatrice wouldn't understand or support her, owing to her strong religious beliefs and pro-life stance. There was also a possibility that she might call the authorities. So, as far as Bernadette was concerned, it just wasn't worth the risk and I eventually respected her choice. When Bernard heard of his aunt's decision not to tell Beatrice, he fully supported it. He said he would deal with the aftermath from his mother when he returned to Ireland.

Anyway, it was now lunchtime, the lists were completed and our hot drinks were finished. It was time for me to head to Rathgar Travel to pick up the tickets for our journey. I parked on Highfield Road and walked the short distance to the travel agent's. I remember it was a lovely warm and sunny day. You could feel a hint of summer in the air. I pushed open the door and stepped inside. There were three or four desks there, all empty except for one. There was a lady I didn't recognise sitting at it. She got up to greet me and asked if she could help. I told her who I was and gave her the name of the girl I had previously dealt with. She politely explained that Caroline was briefly out of the office and asked me to take a seat while I waited for her to return. She reassured me that I wouldn't be waiting too long.

I took a seat. About five minutes later my phone rang. It was my daughter Dawn, and I stepped outside to take the call. Two or three minutes later, while still on the phone, I felt a tap on my shoulder. I lifted my head and turned around. To my horror I saw two gardaí standing behind me. I got an awful fright and explained to my daughter that I would ring her back.

One of the guards asked, 'Are you Gail O'Rorke?' I timidly answered, 'Yes.' In that instant I knew in my heart that they were aware of Bernadette's trip, and that everything had suddenly gone terribly wrong. Time seemed frozen. I couldn't hear anything except the voices in my head and my heart thumping in my ears as my blood pressure rose. I could feel a burning sensation of blind panic rising up through my body. Oh God, I thought, please don't let this be happening.

They asked me to accompany them to Rathmines Garda Station to answer some questions. I had no option but to agree and got into the back of their car. The drive took only about five minutes but seemed much longer. I was terribly upset and I pleaded with them not to stop Bernadette from going on her trip. I kept repeating the same words over and over again, like some kind of lunatic. Nothing made sense.

When we arrived at the station, I was brought to a small, intimidating interview room. The two gardaí were speaking to me in calm voices and were very pleasant. They began by informing me that they did indeed know of my intentions, and told me that my actions regarding Bernadette's journey to Dignitas could be looked upon as an illegal act of assisting in the suicide of another. They told me that this crime carried a maximum prison sentence of fourteen years. They also explained the legal implications of such an act, implications I was unaware of. As far as I was concerned, Bernadette was committing a legal act in a country where it is legal, so how the hell was I in trouble?

They asked me lots of questions about my involvement in organising the trip to Dignitas. I answered as best I could, considering the state I was in. Finally, before they finished the interview, they instructed me to cancel all travel plans with immediate effect. Then they drove me back to my car on Highfield Road. Once alone in my car, I began to sob again. I had to face Bernadette and deliver the devastating news that her well-organised plans and hope of a dignified, peaceful death were shattered. I knew she would already be worried because I had been gone for far too long – the police had kept me for a couple of hours. I truly don't know how I made it to her apartment in one piece – I could barely see where I was going because of the river of tears running down my face. I also felt sick to the pit of my stomach and would have given everything I had in the world to avoid facing her. As I walked through Bernadette's front door she said in an agitated voice, 'Where have you been all this time?'

I sat down in front of her and struggled to get the words out. Taking a deep breath, I tried to explain the events of the past few hours. As I expected, she became very upset. 'Why? No!' she repeated over and over again. I could see that her mind was racing, trying to figure out who had informed the guards of her intended actions. Maybe it was Beatrice, but how had she found out? Or was it the travel agent? Her upset soon turned to anger. 'How dare anyone stop me from doing what I choose to do!' she shouted. 'Who has the right to take away what way I choose to end my life? It's none of their bloody business!'

We sat together for the next while, me trying to soothe Bernadette, and her desperately trying to figure out if there were any other options available to her. The comfort and security of Dignitas was all she ever needed and therefore she had never made other enquiries. Now, the one thing she had put so much store by was gone, and she was frantic that it would not signal the end of the line. She mentioned watching an episode of *The Late Late Show* on RTÉ. A man called Philip Nitschke, who was the founder of an organisation called Exit International, had been a guest. Apparently, Exit was an organisation that ran workshops and also provided information on safe ways of dying with dignity. Bernadette opened her laptop to look up their website. While browsing, she saw the name of the Irish representative, a man called Tom Curran. Bernadette made a note of it and continued browsing. In order to gather the information she needed, Bernadette followed the instructions on how to download an e-book called *The Peaceful Pill Handbook*.

At this stage, I was observing everything from

a distance. I had already come too close to getting myself into serious hot water with the police, and I was filled with trepidation about having any involvement in further arrangements. I was more than happy at this stage to take a back seat. From what I saw of the e-book, its contents were surreal to say the least. There were pictures of various gases and chemicals you could use to end your life, and within the interactive pages was a video of an elderly woman who was talking about placing a large balloon filled with gas over her head as part of the end-of-life procedure. On another page was a photograph of a man holding a large piece of white cardboard in front of him, with his name, address and e-mail address on it. Bernadette explained that he was a Mexican named Dorian Galeazzi and that he was someone from whom you could order substances to end your life. Bernadette made no decision immediately in relation to what option she would ultimately choose. All she decided was to contact Tom Curran.

Bernadette duly got in touch with Tom and it was arranged that he would call two or three days later. On the evening he was scheduled to come, I spoke to him briefly on the phone to give him directions to Bernadette's apartment. When he arrived, I took an instant liking to him. He had a warm demeanour and friendly face. Tom, Bernadette and I sat for a short time in Bernadette's bedroom, talking. Then I left them to talk privately and waited in the living room. I don't know the details of what was said, but I do know that their conversation gave Bernadette great comfort. They shared a lot of similar heartaches: Tom's partner Marie Fleming was in the later stages of multiple sclerosis, so he truly understood Bernadette's dilemma.

Tom was visibly upset leaving the apartment. However, Bernadette seemed calmer and more focused. Bernadette made it clear that she was going ahead with her plan no matter what; there was no stopping her. She decided she was going to contact Dorian Galeazzi and buy a barbiturate called Nembutal, a substance which is banned in Ireland. The first thing Bernadette had to do though was to set up a Hushmail account, which was apparently a secure way of corresponding. After this was done, an initial email was sent and the tense wait for a reply began.

Over the following days there was a rapid deterioration in Bernadette's health. It was as if she was giving up a little more with each passing day. There were undignified aspects to her illness that she never wanted to face. The light at the end of the tunnel for her, in the form of Dignitas, had given her the strength to go as far as this journey required. When the trip to Switzerland fell through, it had a devastating effect on her. Complete exhaustion set in and she was in constant pain and great discomfort. What little appetite she had was fading. Several coffees and one small meal a day was all she could manage. She was paler and weaker than I had ever seen her before.

To her great relief, Dorian Galeazzi made contact and emails were sent back and forth between them. She struggled to compose the messages but knew that she must write them herself to avoid trouble for me. Dorian gave Bernadette instructions on what to do, and furnished her with an address to send the money to. Bernadette was so happy that a new door had opened after one had been slammed shut.

Days passed and I continued to look after Bernadette. I took care of all her needs, both inside and outside her home. At night, when I wasn't with her, she would ring to talk regularly because her nerves were shredded and she often needed the reassurance of a voice at the other end of the phone. She was now totally incontinent. The nightmare of the commode and the struggle for her to adjust to it was a luxury not afforded to her anymore. Her upper body strength had become so diminished that lifting herself up was torture. The indignity of this broke her heart. But like all the obstacles she and I found before us, we got over them with love and, most importantly, with a sense of humour.

With the increase in Bernadette's disability I spent more and more hours with her, and less time at home with my family. The stress had a significant effect on my own health. I wasn't sleeping or eating properly and I was even starting to lose my hair. Barry became very worried and one night, after many protests from me, he insisted that I ask Catherine for help in caring for Bernadette. He said I couldn't do it all on my own, and I knew he was right. However, I was afraid of upsetting Bernadette. I was her carer and she relied on me and was comfortable with our routines – I felt like I was letting her down by asking for help, but I knew I really needed it. Catherine agreed to come to Dublin from Roscommon, to look after her sister one or two days a week. She would stay the night so I could go home and spend some much-needed time with my family. I loved these days; they were so precious. I could relax because I knew someone was taking care of Bernadette, and it also gave me the opportunity to recharge my batteries.

About a week after contact was made with Dorian in Mexico, I returned one day to Bernadette's apartment after running some errands for her. She was very distressed. She said that there was something she needed to tell me and I was going to be upset with her. It took her ages to get the words out. She eventually explained that one of the errands I had done for her was to send the money to Dorian. I almost fainted with the fright. I had gone to the post office for her, and yes,

I'd bought and posted a money order, but I thought it was to purchase something related to angel products because of the name. She was an angel fanatic and the money order was made out to an 'angel' something-or-other. I'm not sure why the name was different, maybe it was a safety issue. I hadn't batted an eye at sending it because I was distracted with a dozen other things on the to-do list. It took a while for me to calm down, but as she talked and explained her dilemma, I began to understand. She basically had no other choice. Going to the post office wasn't something she could do herself because she was housebound, and Catherine didn't run errands for her, so I was her only option.

She also knew that if I'd known what it was, there was a very strong chance I would have refused to post it. How could I stay angry with her? How could I be annoyed at this desperate woman sitting before me? Yes, she had put me in danger, but hers was the greater need. I completely understood, so I gave her a hug and did my best to stop her from crying. At the back of my mind I dreaded going home because I knew that when I told Barry about this, he was going to go ballistic! His main role was to keep me safe, and this one simple act had definitely put me over the line of danger in relation to the guards and the laws on assisting a suicide. My instincts were correct: Barry was furious with Bernadette when I told him.

For now, all we could do was wait for the package to arrive from Mexico. As a result of the immense stress Bernadette was experiencing, her body deteriorated even more. It was literally shutting down. She was in constant pain and, although she was on various medications to help alleviate her discomfort, they weren't helping. To make matters worse, she couldn't sleep. Every single day was torture and she grew increasingly agitated. I dreaded leaving her apartment every night, but I just couldn't be there all the time. Every evening before I left, I would make her as comfortable as possible, ensuring that anything she needed was close at hand. We continued to talk regularly throughout the night on the phone, and this simple act of distraction helped her greatly.

Another thing that had to be arranged was Bernadette's funeral. At her request I phoned Massey's funeral directors and spoke to a lovely woman called Mary, explaining the situation. I put my phone onto loudspeaker so Bernadette could talk and give instructions. She wanted a Humanist service, white lilies and an environmentally friendly coffin. Bernadette was always a great believer in recycling and saving the planet, something that was even reflected in her funeral arrangements. She settled on a wicker coffin called 'The Hyacinth'. She then chose three songs to be played during different parts of her service: the first was 'Living Doll' by Sir Cliff Richard, the second was 'My Favourite

Waste of Time' by Owen Paul, and the third was 'Take It Easy' by The Eagles. Mary was very helpful guiding us through it all and said that she would ring back in a day or two to confirm everything. Bernadette was very pleased that all was now organised for her funeral.

The package seemed to be taking ages to arrive and Bernadette grew increasingly concerned. She was beside herself with worry. She contacted FedEx by e-mail to check on the package's whereabouts and they gave her a number to track it on its journey. It so happened that at this time there were bad floods in Memphis, Tennessee which was the route the package was taking from Mexico, and Bernadette was worried that it had been washed away. Another possibility in her mind was that, as Queen Elizabeth was due to visit Ireland, the package could have been delayed because of stepped-up security. Her frazzled, exhausted mind was thinking up all sorts of reasons for its delay.

After a fortnight of constant worry, there was a knock at Bernadette's front door. I went to answer it and standing on her doorstep was a man in a FedEx uniform with a small box under his arm which was covered in brown wrapping paper with stickers. As much as we were expecting the delivery, I still got a fright when I saw him standing there. I invited him into the living room, where Bernadette was sitting in her wheelchair. The man was pleasant and amiable, with a big warm smile on his face. He handed her the box and she signed for it on an electronic pad. She and I were aware that all these simple actions had to be done solely by her. Me having knowledge of the contents wasn't a crime, whereas physically accepting or signing for the package was, so I went nowhere near it. Bernadette thanked the man and I showed him to the door.

When I walked back into the living room, I saw that Bernadette had tears of relief streaming down her face. She hugged the box for a few moments before removing its wrappings. She took out the two bottles of Nembutal, each of which had the silhouette of a dog on it. The first thing that went through my mind was the expression she always used: 'Put me down and post me home!' Now in her hands was the very thing to fulfil this request. She gently placed the bottles on a small glass table beside the couch.

It was the calmest and happiest I'd seen her since that devastating day when Dignitas was cancelled. She had regained control. The panic subsided and she relaxed once again. I would be lying if I said that I wasn't happy for her. I knew, more than anyone, what this meant to Bernadette. I had witnessed the daily struggle, the fear, the discomfort and the relentless pain she had to endure. I watched this beautiful, energetic, vibrant woman as she was crushed by what she described as her 'tortured shell of a body'.

Ironically, the knowledge that she had the means at her disposal to end her life, on her own terms, was a lifeline to her.

Believing that time was limited, I felt that I needed to talk once more about other options available to her. I knew how she would react, but I didn't care. I brought up the subject of a care home and tried to explain that not all nursing homes were like the bad ones she had heard about in the past. I suggested that now she had the Nembutal, which had a shelf life of ten years or more, she could bring it to the nursing home with her and leave it stashed in her locker while she decided whether or not she wanted to stay. The conversation made her very angry and, as always, I was dismissed with a wave of her hand. She point-blank refused to entertain the idea, saying there was no way she was going to live out the rest of her tormented life being hoisted in and out of bed, fed through a tube and washed and wiped by strangers. In the end, I ran out of arguments. All they ever resulted in was distress for Bernadette, so I eventually dropped the subject. I already knew this was the reaction I would get, but I also knew deep down that I would sleep more soundly in the knowledge that I continued to offer her other choices.

Days passed and the two intimidating bottles sat ominously on the glass table. I had no idea when she would choose to take them. Funnily enough, what

I now witnessed was someone who had actually found reasons to stay alive a little longer. In reality, Bernadette very much wanted to live and now that the security of the Nembutal had arrived, she refocused on things she wanted to do before she died. Watching the visit of the Queen of England to Ireland was one of them. She loved the Royal family and was overjoyed at the welcome the Queen received from the people of Ireland. Another event she wanted to watch was President Obama's visit to Ireland. Throughout this time, though, her health continued to deteriorate at an alarming rate. Her swallow grew weaker and she would regularly choke while drinking. This was very distressing and frightening for her. She knew that if she waited too long, her ability to ingest the Nembutal could be affected. It was her only option to escape this life, and she was petrified of leaving it too late.

One day, towards the end of May, she sat me down and informed me that she had made her decision. The date chosen was Sunday, 5 June. There was, as always, a practical side to the decision. Bernadette was a huge fan of the show *Britain's Got Talent*, and she very much wanted to watch the final. 'Pip and Puppy' was on it that year and was her favourite act. I suppose you could say it was the last thing on her bucket list. One of the most upsetting things for me personally was that I knew I couldn't sit with her when she ended her life. Being together at the end had previously been part of her plan. However, between the intervention by the gardaí in relation to Dignitas and my current fear of prosecution, it was now not an option to stay with her. I hated this. It broke my heart that I couldn't be there to hold her hand and comfort her while she faced the most frightening thing a person can face: dying.

The decision was made that Barry and I would stay in a hotel in Kilkenny on the night of Sunday, 5 June. Bernadette wanted me far enough away from Dublin that there would be no question about my whereabouts when she carried out her wish. Over the following days I continued to make Bernadette's life as comfortable as possible as she prepared to die with dignity, on her own terms.

7

I got very little sleep on the Saturday night. My mind was awash with fear, worry and a great sadness – not for Bernadette, but selfishly for myself. I knew all that mattered was that she achieve what she desired so greatly, but my stomach was churning with every emotion and my heart was breaking. The emphasis had to be on Bernadette's journey out of her crushed and tortured shell of a body, but I was losing one of the most special people in my life. She had become such a huge part of me through our friendship, and was soon to die. I was struggling to hold myself together. Barry and I sat for hours at our kitchen table on the Sunday morning and all I could do was cry. Barry was being strong but I could see he was also close to breaking point. I knew once I turned the key in Bernadette's front door I would have to put on a brave face but, for now, that was the last thing I could manage.

Eventually I did pull myself together. Barry gave me a huge hug and I left the house to go over to Bernadette's apartment one last time. I arrived there just after 10 a.m. and saw that she was snoozing in her wheelchair with her feet up on the couch. I had placed them there the previous evening before I left, and since she was unable to lift up her legs any more, they had remained in that position all night long. She woke up when I entered the living room and asked me to go to Insomnia and buy her two americano coffees and a hot chocolate for myself. The day started like all other days, both of us sipping our drinks while we chatted about plans for the day ahead. She was very calm and strong.

She asked me to bring her to her bedroom so she could choose an outfit to wear because she wanted to look her best for the visitors who were to arrive later. Catherine and her family were to come over in the afternoon to see her. Then her friend Mary Lundy was to stop by in the early evening to spend some time with her. She chose a beautiful turquoise dress she had bought in Marks and Spencer the previous Christmas, which was loose-fitting and comfortable. Then I helped her to shower, blow-dried her hair and helped her to get dressed. She looked beautiful. In saying that, I couldn't help feeling everything was so surreal.

I savoured each thing we were doing because it would be my last time to do them for her. I also knew these memories would be ones I would hold on to for years to come and I made every minute count. About an hour before her first visitors were due to arrive and after all that was to be done had been completed, we sat together, she in her chair facing me and me sitting on her couch. We held each other's hands and took turns to say all the things we wanted to say to each other.

With tears streaming down our cheeks, I told her how much I loved her. I thanked her for all that she had been to me throughout our friendship, and tried to say how much I was going to miss her. Then it was her turn. She said so many beautiful things that it's impossible to list them. She thanked me for giving her her life back by caring for her the way I had and for doing all I had done over the last few months to help her get to this very day. We talked for about an hour. All I actually wanted to do was wave a magic wand and fix her, so she didn't have to go through with her plan. I wanted her to be well so we could spend many more years in each other's company, enjoying the riches of our friendship. I struggled to compose myself and all the while she was being my rock.

At 3.30 p.m. Catherine and her family arrived and I went outside to greet them. With Catherine were Catriona, her husband Shane and their two children, Kate and Jamie. Soon Bernadette had a big smile on her face and was showing Kate footage from *Britain's Got Talent*, which she had previously recorded on her digital box. 'Pip and Puppy' were featured, much to Bernadette's delight, and she was bursting to show it to Kate. I knew it was time for me to leave; I didn't want to be in the way while her family was there, so I leant down, gave her a great big hug, kissed her on the cheek and quietly told her one last time that I loved her.

Driving home, I felt like a zombie. I walked through my front door, fell into Barry's arms and lost control of every emotion. As ever, he minded me like no other could but I was inconsolable. After about an hour we packed a few things for our journey to Kilkenny and left. We chose Kilkenny because we had stayed there a few times in the past. As we drove, there was very little conversation between us, and we didn't want to turn on the radio.

We arrived at the River Court Hotel around 7.30 p.m. When we checked in, the girl in charge at reception informed us that we had been upgraded to a suite. We found out that Bernadette had made a call to them at some stage over the last day or two requesting it for us. It was the kind of thing she loved to do. I know she had the best of intentions, but I'm afraid on this particular night it was a little wasted. Our room was named The Earl of Ormond suite and was beautifully decorated. We unpacked the few things we had brought and sat for a while to gather our thoughts. The night ahead was inevitably going to be horrendous, knowing what was taking place back in Dublin.

Barry felt it would be a good idea to head into the town centre. He wanted to ensure that we were seen on as many CCTV cameras as possible, thereby eliminating any doubt the authorities might have regarding our whereabouts on that night. We walked for a while holding each other's hands, both of us struggling to seem as normal as we could under the circumstances. We went to Dunnes Stores to grab a few bits and pieces, knowing that there would be in-store cameras that we could be seen on. We then went to a restaurant for something to eat. It was very busy that night, but we just stayed in our own little bubble of numbness, not talking to anyone else. I kept checking the time, wondering what was happening back at Bernadette's apartment. We headed back to the hotel a while later.

When we returned to our hotel room, we ordered a movie: *The King's Speech*. In our frazzled minds we thought that this could, if necessary, prove that we hadn't left the room and sneaked back to Dublin to be with Bernadette. As I type these words, it all seems quite unnecessary, but at the time we thought what we were doing was important. Understandably, neither of us got much sleep that night. I couldn't pick up the phone to ring Bernadette, it would have been too much of a risk. The hours seemed to drag by and yet the morning was coming way too quickly.

I nodded off at around four o'clock but tossed and turned until 8 a.m. when we both got up and got dressed. I kept thinking, oh God, this is it, it's Monday morning. It was arranged that I would ring Bernadette and, if she didn't answer her phone, I was to ring Elizabeth, her friend who lived in the same complex. Elizabeth was a very good neighbour to Bernadette and also a keyholder. I would ask her to check in on Bernadette to see how she was. I don't know what came over me, but once I picked up the phone I suddenly found myself incapable of dialling her number. I simply hadn't the strength to do as I had promised. Half of me hoped so much that she would answer, and the other hoped she wouldn't. A million thoughts ran through my head, which was now thumping because of my rising blood pressure. No matter how I tried, I just could not make the call, so I handed the phone to Barry and asked him to do it.

For a few moments he held the phone out as if it was a lit stick of dynamite. Eventually he dialled her number, and I could hear it ringing and ringing. She didn't answer. I begged him to ring her two or three more times because she might have simply been asleep and didn't hear the phone the first time, but there was still no answer. Then I thought, maybe she had just dropped her phone and couldn't get to it like many times before. We both felt utterly helpless standing in that hotel room. We were so prepared and yet not prepared at all. So I rang Elizabeth, and asked her to check on Bernadette. All she said was, 'No problem, I'll ring you back', before hanging up.

Thankfully we didn't have to wait too long. When Elizabeth called back, she was clearly upset. She told me that Bernadette had passed away. She said that she looked so peaceful and beautiful and appeared twenty years younger, sitting in her wheelchair. These words flooded my brain with happiness for my dear friend. At last she was free; she had escaped the body she had grown to hate so much and I have no doubt that she was already in heaven dancing with her father. She had achieved her ultimate goal: to die with dignity. I was overwhelmed with emotion and felt an enormous sense of inner peace.

We agreed that Elizabeth would ring the police, so she hung up and within a few minutes rang me back to say this was done. After our call ended, Barry and I packed our things, checked out of the hotel and began making our way back to Dublin. Elizabeth rang me twice more while we were on our way home to keep me updated. She told me that the gardaí were at Bernadette's apartment and that Catherine and Bernadette's friend Mary were there too. I'm not too sure what time we got back home but I knew that, no matter what, I could not go near Bernadette's home. It greatly upset me leaving everything for others to do, but I was so afraid and couldn't even ring anyone. I remember getting a call from Catherine, who was beside herself with grief.

A few days later I received a call from the police. The officer introduced himself as Garda Andrew Dermody and he asked if Barry and I could call into Donnybrook station for an informal interview. He was very friendly and we agreed to come in the following day. We were both highly nervous but knew it had to be done. When we arrived, we were brought into a small interview room. I remember commenting on the garda's age, as he seemed too young to be a member of the force. He was nice and we warmed to him quickly. He asked us a variety of questions, nothing out of the ordinary. They were mostly about Bernadette and my relationship with her, and we answered as many questions as we could. The interview didn't last very long. The garda thanked us for coming and left us to the door. Little did we know I would be seeing a great deal more of the inside of Donnybrook Garda Station in the near future.

Bernadette's funeral was a couple of days later. Catriona and her husband Shane made any last arrangements which Bernadette and I hadn't finalised. The funeral took place in Newlands Cross crematorium, where they cater for humanist services. When my extended family and I arrived, there was quite a good crowd already gathered. The day was warm and sunny, and inside the temple it was beautiful, airy and bright, exactly what Bernadette would have wanted. As we walked through the main door, our eyes were drawn to the columns of red balloons which lined the walls. After asking around, we couldn't find out who had ordered them. The only conclusion we could come to was that Bernadette had ordered them herself before she died. This didn't surprise me. The pale wicker coffin she had chosen was gorgeous, and adorned with pure white lilies. It made me so happy to know that her final wishes had been respected.

The readings at the service were not religious, just personal heartfelt words from people who had loved Bernadette deeply. I read one myself. A month earlier Elizabeth had taken me to one side in the car park of Bernadette's apartment complex and handed me a sheet of paper. She asked me if it would be something I would like to read when the time came. Written on the top of the page were the words, 'Here she comes,' followed by the most beautiful text relating to a person's passing. It spoke of the sadness of losing someone close, but, more importantly, of the joy experienced by those in the afterlife as they watched them arrive. I felt honoured to be asked to speak at her funeral and now I had in my hands exactly what I wanted to say.

I am standing on the sea shore. Suddenly a ship at my side spreads her white sails to the morning breeze and starts out for the ocean. She is an object of beauty and courage. I stand and watch her until at length she is only a ribbon of white cloud – just above where the sea and sky mingle with each other.

Then someone at my side says, 'There, she's gone!'

'Gone where?'

'Gone from my sight, that is all.'

She is just as large in mast and hull as she was when she left my side – and just as able to bear her load of living freight to the place of her destination. Her diminished size is in me, not in her, for just at that moment, when someone at my side says, 'There, she's gone,' there are other voices ready to greet her, with a glad shout, 'Look, here she comes!'

During the service the songs chosen by Bernadette were played. As we all walked out to the strains of 'Take It Easy' by The Eagles, we were each handed a red balloon. We made our way into the warm sunshine and were guided towards a grassy area. We stood side by side and at the same time released our red balloons. It was a truly beautiful moment: the balloons were lifted up by the gentle June breeze – well, all except one, which became temporarily stuck in a nearby tree. We all laughed and watched as the wind dislodged it and it floated off in a different direction to the others. It was so symbolic. That one lone red balloon doing it differently, determined not to follow the crowd. We all felt that this rebel balloon represented Bernadette. She too forged her own path, and it was a special moment shared by everyone that day, something I will never forget. After the service, we went to a nearby hotel for tea and sandwiches. It was a very sad but successful day and I just knew Bernadette was smiling down from heaven on all of us.

8

After Bernadette's funeral, Barry and I took a much-needed couple of weeks off work. We were both physically and mentally exhausted. Everything over the past six months, all that we had gone through as a couple and a family, had taken its toll. We needed to rest and attempt to get back to some kind of normality. I found adjusting to life without Bernadette quite difficult. For such a long time we were practically joined at the hip, and now I felt an emptiness that couldn't be filled. I had many mixed feelings. I wanted so much to grieve for the loss of one of the closest people in my life, but every time I began to feel sad, there was a voice inside my head telling me to stop being so selfish. It constantly reminded me of the peace and happiness I truly believed Bernadette was experiencing. I believed she had got her wish that she would dance in heaven on her new, healthy legs. For a while this partly overshadowed my own feelings of sadness. But, under all the logic and compassion, no matter how hard I tried, my grief remained, and I missed her terribly.

Well my name is Bernadette Forde and my date of birth is 16/08/59 and I have MS. I'm progressive for ten years diagnosed but it has got very bad in the last number of months and I knew it was getting bad so I had made arrangements to go to Dignitas in Zurich but then my hopes were dashed, because the police got to my friend when she went to collect the tickets and I hadn't realised until then that Gail and Bernard my nephew were going to get into difficulty for assisting even though they weren't actually assisting at all, they were just going to travel with me to Zurich. But anyway when I realised that was what was happening I no longer wanted that because I didn't want Gail or Mary or anyone around anymore if they were going to get into trouble for it because I left it so that I wouldn't

*have anyone after that happened – Dignitas – but
I knew what I needed to do because I can't, I just
can't live with this anymore, it's just my life is
shit and I just can't keep going with everything,
with trying to get to the loo with pads, with seats,
everything is just a nightmare and, but, after the
Dignitas experience I realised I had to do whatever
I did alone, that I can't even talk to anyone in case
they are implicated, so no help at all now and it is
very difficult that I can't even talk to anyone. So the
first thing I did after Dignitas was to go online and
see what help I could get and what I had seen on
a programme on the* Late Late *and online I found
the Exit International Website and started looking
up from that what I could do and I eventually
managed to get hold of this stuff from Mexico. I
was able to order it online and it was delivered to
me by courier, but that took over two weeks to get
here and it's just so difficult that, you know, I just
can't do any of this again or anymore. Like I said,
hiding it from friends has been difficult, it's just so
unfair that I have to, that I can't contact or chat to
anyone, that I have to be totally alone. But anyway
that's just it so as I said I got the stuff from Mexico
and I do intend to do it but I can't let, as I said,
I can't let anyone know so as soon, I actually got
this Dictaphone online, Pete's of Parnell Square
or whatever, so I have the stuff for the guards or*

whatever and the receipt and instructions of how to use it, so you know because my writing is very bad so actually a suicide note might not be possible so that's why I'm using this and I hope that it will make my wishes, my intentions clear to anyone who wants to question it afterwards, because it's me and totally me and nobody else and you know I suppose I'm just very frustrated it has to be this way. I mean why it has to be like this in Ireland and you know I couldn't get to Dignitas where it all could have been done you know. Oh I'm sorry, I'm just, I think I've said all I'm going to say for now.

On the day of Bernadette's funeral, Catherine and I discussed where her ashes were going. She informed me that they were being placed in her father's grave in County Longford. This is something Bernadette would have chosen had she been there to make the decision. She adored her dad; it was only right that they rest side by side. Catherine told me that she would be in touch to make arrangements with me regarding travelling down to Longford to be a part of the service.

My phone rang late one night soon after, around 11 p.m. It was Catherine. There was a discomfort in her tone, and it sounded as if she was struggling to say what she had to say to me. When the words eventually came out, it was to tell me that the service to bury Bernadette's ashes had taken place that very day. I couldn't believe what I was hearing! My stomach tensed. Why had I not been invited? Why the bloody hell did I not get a call from anyone about it? I became very upset. I questioned why she didn't ring me to tell me, but she couldn't give me a direct answer. It didn't take me long to put two and two together. I knew that Bernadette's sister Beatrice had never liked me and there was no doubt in my mind that the decision to exclude me was hers. Of this I had no proof but I knew how she worked, how much control she loved to have.

I had already experienced that control around the time of the crash, when I had been prevented from seeing Bernadette in the aftermath. Now, here I was again, excluded from something that I very much wanted to be part of. I was gutted. All I had ever done was love and care for their sister. They had witnessed the loyalty and commitment I gave throughout my friendship with her. They saw how happy she was, and they knew that having someone to rely on had extended her life. And this is how they had decided to treat me? I had no choice but to suck it up. What else could I do? Before hanging up the phone, Catherine sincerely apologised, and through my upset and anger, I could see that she truly meant it. Whatever was behind it, it wasn't her fault.

Over the following weeks I received a couple of

phone calls from the guards in Donnybrook, who informed me that they had begun an investigation into Bernadette's death. At the time this seemed standard procedure, so I wasn't fazed. They asked me to drop a number of items into the station relating to Bernadette. This included some paperwork and a small green notepad that I had used when writing lists of instructions from Bernadette. Nothing out of the ordinary.

Towards the end of September I received another call from the gardaí. This time they asked me to come to Donnybrook for an interview. I was fine with that because I wanted to help in any way I could. Bernadette had died, I was the closest person to her in the last months of her life, so it made sense the guards would have questions that needed to be answered. It was agreed that I would come in on Thursday, 29 September at 10.30 a.m. Barry drove me there and said he would wait outside in the car, no matter how long it took. He comforted me with reassuring words. 'Just tell the truth, Gail,' he said, and gave me a big 'Barry' hug before walking me to the door. Even though I truly felt I had done no wrong, it didn't stop me from trembling with nerves. Once inside the building I was shown to a small interview room by a member of staff. The room was like something from *The Bill*, an old show off the telly. It had dirty, pale blue walls and an old wooden desk, which had a single seat on one side and two on the other. The one small window was heavily secured with iron bars. If I'm honest, I found it all quite intimidating. I was interviewed by Detective Inspector Sean Campbell and Detective Jim Byrne. I liked one more than the other straight away. Detective Byrne adopted a friendly demeanour and went out of his way to make me feel comfortable. The inspector, on the other hand, scared the pants off me. He seemed emotionless and had a rather cold stare. I felt uneasy around him. I guess it was the 'good cop, bad cop' routine we are all familiar with from watching television. The first words they spoke were daunting. They said, 'You are not obliged to say anything, but anything you do say may be used in evidence'! My stomach somersaulted.

Never in my life did I think I would find myself in a situation where I would hear these words. The seriousness of the situation had definitely been turned up a notch or two. They then began asking me all about how I came to meet Bernadette, the when's, how's and why's. They asked me about the car crash we were involved in back in 2008 and enquired about Bernadette's dexterity and physical abilities. Could she use a computer? Hold a cup unaided? With every question they asked, the knot in my stomach grew tighter. Where were they going with this?

They asked all about Dignitas. Who had made the initial contact? Who had emailed them? The questions seemed endless. All my answers were written down and also videoed by a camera that was bolted to the wall behind their heads. Panic rose inside me, but I did my best to hide the worry I was feeling. I knew in my heart that I had done nothing wrong. At 1.30 p.m. they allowed me to take a short break. It had been only three hours, but I was already exhausted. Barry and I got a bite of lunch and I returned about an hour later.

The second phase of questioning began at 2.22 p.m. They started by asking me about Bernadette's finances and her pension. I kept telling myself that this was all normal and that they were just trying to eliminate the chance that someone may have gained financially from her death. They had a job to do and I fully respected that. The next line of questioning was about Exit International. How did Bernadette know of the organisation? Who else knew about it? How had she made contact? There were so many questions, my head was spinning.

Then they asked me the question I feared the most. About the money transfer to Mexico. I began to feel sick with anxiety. I knew the truth behind the transaction, that Bernadette had been left with no choice but to deceive me – but would they believe me? After asking me, Inspector Campbell reached down beside him and from a file he took out a small piece of paper. It was the receipt from Western

Union. I explained, as best I could, how Bernadette had no choice but to deceive me in her attempt to source what she so desperately needed. Again, they wrote my answers in their big book and continued interrogating me. I was growing increasingly sore and tense sitting on the hard chair, which was bolted to the floor.

More and more questions. As I talked, they were writing up my statement. I did my best to compose myself since there seemed no end in sight to their relentless questioning. Many more hours were spent in that small, cold and uncomfortable room. At 7 p.m. the gruelling ordeal finally ceased. My brain was numb and my body was sore, but I was free to go at last. I was an emotional wreck and sobbed all the way home in the car.

A couple of days later Barry was asked to come in for an interview at Donnybrook station. It was 3 October 2011. This interview lasted for two and a half hours and mainly covered the same questions that I had already been asked.

A day or two later I received yet another request to come in for an interview. I was worried all over again. Had I not already answered everything for them? What more did they need to know? As always, I was cooperative, and the interview was arranged for Friday, 7 October. It was basically more of the same: questions about Dignitas, Bernadette's finances, my role in Bernadette's life on a daily basis. Thankfully it lasted only one hour but, again, I left fearing the consequences of my innocent actions. I was afraid that they were trying to pin something on me that I clearly hadn't done. Your head goes to strange places when you are that scared. You overthink until you almost lose your mind. If it wasn't for Barry's constant support, I honestly don't know how I would have coped. The impact all this stress was having on my mental well-being was beginning to show. I was finding it increasingly difficult to sleep and when I did drop off, my dreams were dark and scary. My hair was now falling out at an alarming rate, and I had new bald patches forming on a monthly basis. My mind was consumed with worry. I wondered if the latest interview was the last one, and tried to guess who else was being questioned and what their story was. Would they also tell the truth, or would they make things up to protect their own backsides? This guessing game was driving me mad. The thing was, I was unable to contact anyone because the gardaí gave me specific instructions not to do so. For now, I had to do my best to get my head together and put all this craziness to one side in an attempt to get on with my normal life.

In the midst of all this madness, while sitting at home one evening with Barry, I received a phone call from my brother Steve. After many years of ups and downs in relation to my parents, Steve was the only one of my siblings who still regularly saw them and he was ringing me to let me know that my mother was in hospital dying from cancer. He wanted to give me the opportunity to see her one last time before she died.

If I am brutally honest, I truly didn't know how to feel. I didn't have any real feelings towards her and although I have immense sympathy for anyone going through such an ordeal, the call didn't have the impact that maybe it should have had on a daughter, hearing that her mam was soon to die. I thanked Steve for letting me know and told him that I would have to think about what I was going to do. For more than twenty years, my life had greatly improved due to the absence of my mother. I also knew that going to see her would be like playing a game of Russian roulette. There was an ever so small chance that she might be remorseful and say the right thing, but the mother I knew could and maybe would take the opportunity to have one last dig, thereby leaving me to regret visiting her forever. I really was torn as to how to handle this new situation. I rang my sister Linda to tell her what had happened. She too was taken aback but felt exactly as I did.

I had not seen my mother in almost twenty years. I thought of her from time to time, and there were two occasions over the years when there was an attempt at some kind of a reunification. But, in truth, there was little if any loving connection between us and ultimately these meetings didn't lead to any rekindling of love – perhaps because the flame had never really been there to begin with – or had been blown out too soon by bitter circumstances.

Over time, one by one and for a variety of reasons, my siblings had severed contact with my parents, apart from Steve. I cherished my relationships with all of my siblings – we were survivors of a merciless household who thankfully had only become closer as a result of it. But, for me, time had not lessened the wounds inflicted on me by my parents. In fact, if anything, my childhood only became more painful to me as the years went on.

And my mother was at the heart of that pain. Although I could only imagine what she herself must have endured being married to a brute of a man like my father, nonetheless I had had to separate from her to survive because, as I saw it, my mother, rather than protecting us, had sacrificed us to him, protecting herself. As a mother myself, whose instinct was only ever to protect my kids from harm, it was not something I could ever understand, let alone forgive. And now, faced with the inevitability of her passing, I felt as though I was standing on a precipice. Going to see her meant taking a big leap – and I was terrified.

A day or two passed and I received a call from my daughter Dawn. She told me that she was in the lift of the hospital where my mother was. She was with my brother Steve and she was going to visit the grandmother she had never known. I raised my children to be independent, strong people, so I was not surprised – this was her decision and I respected it.

The reception she received when they met was thankfully a good one and left Dawn with no regrets. But knowing how Mam handled it made me even more confused as to what to do myself, so I agreed that if Linda and I went together I would go. Unfortunately, however, my mother threw a spanner in the works because she refused to see Linda. This was upsetting enough, and in solidarity I dug my heels in once again and cancelled the visit.

Another few days passed and my mother was moved to Our Lady's Hospice in Harold's Cross. I talked on and off with Linda, still not knowing what to do, but eventually came to the decision that I would go. Either way, there was a great risk of regret, so I opted for the scarier choice. I travelled there with Steve, my heart full to the brim with emotion and a childlike fear. I hadn't seen her for so long, would she even recognise me? I feared the wrath of an angry, dying woman and what words she might throw at me, but that wasn't what greeted me as I approached her bed. When her head turned and our eyes met, they weren't the same eyes I had known from the past. There was a softness and warmth in them which I had never seen before and her entire face lit up when she saw me. I nervously said, 'Hi, Mam,' and smiled. I sat beside her on the bed and she took hold of my hand and just kept saying the words 'I love you' over and over as if she was trying to make up for all the years that she had never told me. We were both crying. For the first time in my life I saw my mother as a frail, vulnerable woman who now, so close to meeting her maker, had let go of the anger and cruelty that had taken over her heart and soul. We talked about life and about my little family. She told me how amazing and beautiful Dawn was and how happy she was that she had come to see her. It was the first time my mother had ever made me feel proud of my achievements. I simply could not stop crying, nor could she.

It is so strange how an anger which had consumed me for almost two decades simply faded away in those precious few moments. Everything I felt in the past was gone in the blink of an eye, something I never thought possible. I was so happy that I had gone to see her. She knew in her heart that she had made a mess of her life, and ours, be it her fault or my father's, but seeing her recognise these facts and trying so hard in the short time she had left to make amends was all I needed to forgive her. I stayed for a while longer, we talked, shared a few happy moments and said goodbye. I told her that I loved her too before leaving. My mother passed away three days later and was laid to rest in Bluebell cemetery, which is a stone's throw from where she grew up.

I believe strongly in an afterlife and that my mam is now among the angels whom I talk to almost daily. My belief is that wherever she is, she sees everything past and present and I feel that she helps guide me through my life here on earth. My father wasn't at her funeral. By then he was in a nursing home, in the early stages of dementia. He will be eighty-five on his next birthday and as my siblings and I often say, not even the devil wants him.

Over the following weeks and months everything was quiet: no calls from the gardaí, no interviews. My mind began to relax a little more with each passing day. Christmas came and went, then springtime, and still nothing. My hope and belief that the investigation was over grew stronger. But in July 2012 I received yet another call requesting me to come in to Donnybrook Garda Station. I was gutted and more worried than ever.

Once again I made the nervous journey to the station, with Barry by my side as always. It was Wednesday 11 July. The interview began at 12.49 p.m. This time I was questioned by Detective Byrne and a female colleague, Detective Sinead O'Connor.

Again their questions covered much the same ground as before. I thought that maybe they were seeing if my answers varied from previous ones; were they trying to trip me up? This didn't worry me too much because the truth remains the truth, no matter how much time passes. While sitting in that dull, cold room, I wondered how the really 'bad guys' cope under the stress and pressure. I now fully understood why the chair was firmly bolted to the floor. At 5.42 p.m. the interview came to an end. There had been no surprises, no new questions. All things considered, this was the least stressful session so far. It may have been because I was a little more used to it by now, or maybe it was simply that the intimidating Inspector Campbell's replacement in the form of the lovely Detective O'Connor made it more bearable. But whatever the reason, I was glad this interview didn't knock the wind out of me like all the other ones had done. I have to say I was relieved and overjoyed when I left that building, and I fervently prayed it would be the very last time I would have to go there.

9

Months passed without so much as a whisper from the gardaí and I allowed myself to relax a little more. I began to believe that the investigation had come to an end and that maybe the guards had at last come to the rightful conclusion that Bernadette had taken her own life. It was so lovely to have some peace of mind after all the stress of the last couple of years.

Christmas arrived, bringing with it the wonderful news that I was going to be a grandmother. My son Aaron and his partner Laura told me they were expecting a baby the following July. We were overjoyed. To our surprise, a fortnight later our daughter Dawn arrived at our house looking a little shell-shocked, informing us that she and her partner Adam were expecting a baby too. I could not believe it – two beautiful little angels coming into our lives! We felt so blessed. These two fantastic pieces of news were just the tonic to take my mind off all the police interviews and endless worry.

Baylee Freya O'Rorke, Aaron's daughter, came into our world on 20 July 2013. She was a beautiful, healthy, blue-eyed angel who stole our hearts. I remember sitting in our living room with Barry and my sister Linda as we eagerly waited for news. When the first photo of the newly born little bundle came through, we danced around the house and garden with happiness. She was so perfect. She was barely out of the womb and already looked like she was wearing a big smile on her little face.

Four short weeks later Samia Mai Solimann was born. Dawn went through the mill giving birth and when our second little angel was born, she was battered and bruised. But even though Samia was very small and fragile, she was perfect in every way and absolutely gorgeous. Barry and I felt like the luckiest people in the world to have been given the priceless gift of two beautiful granddaughters.

When you are a parent, you worry constantly about

your children, truly believing that there is no worry in the world like it. But watching your children become parents themselves teaches you that you were wrong. It brings worry to a whole new level. With the luck of the gods, Barry and I managed to raise two strong, confident, kind and sensible children, both of whom were in long-term relationships. It was such a pleasure to watch the two couples taking to parenting so naturally.

In September Aaron and Laura hosted Baylee's christening. It was a fantastic day, made all the more wonderful when Aaron got down on bended knee with Baylee on his lap wearing a bib which read, 'Mammy, will you marry my Daddy?' to which she thankfully replied yes. Samia's christening was on 17 November. Again, it was a fantastic day filled with family and fun. Samia was still so tiny and looked beautiful in her little cream dress. Both christenings were days to be treasured.

Tuesday, 19 November 2013, two days after Samia's christening, began like any average day. Barry and I had taken a few days off work and Aaron was bringing Baylee for a visit in the afternoon. We were sitting at the kitchen table having a chat and a cup of tea when my mobile phone rang. Detective Jim Byrne's number showed on the screen. As I went to answer it, I saw Aaron coming into the garden with Baylee in his arms, so I ran upstairs to the quietness of my bedroom to take the call. I thought that maybe he was ringing to tell me that the investigation was finally over.

'Hi Jim, how are you?'

His tone of voice was not what I expected. He meekly said hello and then uttered the words I will never forget: 'Gail, I am so sorry. They have charged you.' I cannot begin to describe the next few moments. I felt as though I had been punched in the stomach. The only word I could get out was 'No'. I just kept repeating it over and over again and screamed out for Barry, struggling to hold the phone in my hand. He came running up the stairs, and I cried, 'They've charged me, they've charged me,' before throwing my phone at him in a blind panic.

I lost my ability to speak, and all that would come out were screams. My legs went from underneath me and I collapsed onto the floor. I managed to get to my knees and through my bedroom window I could see Barry standing at our garden gate talking on the phone. He was crying and visibly shaking while talking to Jim. Within a minute or two I collapsed again. When Barry was finished on the phone, he ran up the stairs again and tried to help me up. But I wasn't able to find the strength to stand, and I couldn't stop crying and screaming. Aaron then came into the room and got down on his knees in front of me, holding both my hands in his. He stared into my eyes, trying to get me to focus.

Eventually my screams stopped long enough for Aaron to get me to my feet. I was still trembling all over and unable to breathe properly. He walked me slowly down the stairs to where I saw Barry waiting with Baylee in his arms. He handed her back to Aaron and then wrapped his strong arms around me. The following few hours are, unsurprisingly, something of a blur. I was consumed with terror and panic, and didn't know which end was up. All through that day we had many concerned visitors calling to offer their support. I was very grateful for all the help but their efforts went almost unnoticed because my mind couldn't focus on anything. I simply could not see any light at the end of the very dark tunnel that Jim Byrne's call had thrown me into. I struggled to get any kind of grip on my emotions, and all I could think about was the punishment of prison for being a true and loyal friend. How had things ended up this way?

One by one everyone left until there was just Barry, Aaron, Dawn, Laura and me. I eventually stopped crying and we sat as calmly as we could and discussed the situation. Barry told me that while he was on the phone to Jim, he had agreed that I would present myself at Donnybrook Garda Station the following day where they would formally arrest and charge me. I felt sick to the pit of my stomach. Where was I going to find the strength to face this when I was feeling as weak as a kitten?

I got little or no sleep that night, which in itself was a blessing, because every time I did drift off, my dreams were dark and scary. The next morning I was still on the edge of panic, finding it hard to catch my breath. Barry must have hugged me a hundred times or more; he was amazing and helped me gain the strength and courage I needed to just walk out my front door. To my relief, Aaron came with us, since Barry was going to need support of his own while I was detained.

When we arrived at the station, Aaron waited in the car. I remember walking along the pathway at the side of the old garda station with its dark-bricked walls and ominous appearance, thinking maybe we could just keep walking and not stop. Or maybe we could get back into the car and head for the airport and run away. But both of us knew that I had to face this situation, like it or not.

I wasn't running away from this. I had no idea what lay ahead of me, but in my heart and, more importantly, in my soul, I knew I had done nothing wrong. I was very honoured to be a part of Bernadette's life and in many ways a part of her death. I was proud of who I was and the role I had played, so I held my head high, put on my bravest face and walked trembling into the front office of the garda station. Barry notified the female officer at the desk of who we were and who wanted to see us, and she went off to inform the investigating officer. We sat together on the wooden bench. I was holding on to Barry, afraid to let go, in case I collapsed again. While we waited, a couple of people came in requesting forms for various things, passports and the like. Time dragged by with no sign of Jim Byrne. Before long, my newfound strength disappeared and I began to have a huge anxiety attack. Because this was something I had never experienced before, I was convinced I was having a heart attack. I began to hyperventilate and was close to vomiting. At one point a very concerned man offered words of advice to Barry about what I should do to alleviate the symptoms. I must have been some sight crying and shaking, but I just couldn't stop it.

After what felt like hours, a door to our right opened. Jim was standing there with that familiar soft look on his face. I was so relieved it was he who was there to greet us. We stood up and Barry walked me through the door and into a small, narrow hallway. I was still in tears. Barry said to Jim, 'You look after her, Jim. You mind my baby.' To which Jim replied, 'I will, Barry, I promise.' Barry hugged me one last time before being escorted out. I was suddenly overcome by the realisation that I couldn't leave. As an adult you can always leave a situation if you really want to but here I was, not a free woman any more, and as the door closed between Barry and me, it really hit home. It was one of the scariest and most uncomfortable feelings I have ever experienced.

Accompanying Jim was a female guard. She too was very friendly towards me and, not unlike Jim, had a reassuring look on her face. They offered me a seat while I waited to be formally charged. About fifteen minutes later I was shown into another room where the station sergeant was sitting behind a big old desk. I couldn't help feeling like a bold schoolchild being sent to await the wrath of the school principal. I felt about two feet tall. In front of him on his desk was a huge book. He began by asking me to remove all my jewellery. Silly as it sounds, my jewellery is an integral part of who I am. After I handed everything to him, I felt quite naked and greatly humiliated. The sergeant even requested the removal of clips and bobbins from my hair. I'm not too sure what damage he felt I could have done to myself or someone else with a hair bobbin, but I respected their rules and did as he asked.

Then he picked up his pen and began asking me questions, the answers to which he wrote in his very large book. After several questions he paused, looked straight into my eyes and said, 'Gail O'Rorke, you have been charged with assisting in the suicide of Bernadette Forde. Do you have anything to say?' For a moment I panicked. My brain went into meltdown and I found myself saying, 'Guilty'. He stared at me and repeated my answer. I looked at him, realising what I had said and almost shouted the words, 'I mean not guilty, oh my God, I mean not guilty!' Fortunately, that was what he wrote down. When he was finished asking me all his questions, he handed me over to another female officer. I walked to a waiting garda car outside, flanked on either side by Jim Byrne and two officers. I couldn't see Barry anywhere in the car park. I wasn't sure if he had gone on ahead to meet me at the court.

I sat in the back with one of the female officers while Jim and another female officer sat in the front. They explained that we were heading to the Criminal Courts of Justice. They told me that the media had got wind of my arrest and would more than likely be waiting for us. Jim said they were going to try to get me there before the media had a chance to gather. I couldn't believe what I was hearing. The media? What the hell was going on?

The journey was terrifying. Since the car crash in 2008, I had become a really bad passenger at the best of times. And now a guard was driving, with sirens blaring, faster than I had ever experienced. It was like something you would see in a movie. We drove at breakneck speed, forcing our way through stationary traffic, not even stopping at red traffic lights. I could see pedestrians and motorists glaring our way and trying to get a glimpse of whomever was in the back seat. All I could do was keep my head down and pray that we didn't crash.

As we approached the Courts of Justice, I could see two or three photographers waiting at the top of the steps. Our attempt to beat them had failed. We pulled up right outside the building and, as I stepped from the car, the cameramen went crazy, clicking away. I didn't know where to look. How in God's name did they even know who I was? I walked up the steps as quickly as I could and in through the glass double doors. Even as a taxi driver passing it many times a week, I never paid it much attention; I had never had cause to until now. Bigger on the inside than the outside would suggest, the building has many floors and a huge, circular space in the middle. As we entered the lobby, my eyes searched frantically for Barry and Aaron but they were nowhere to be seen.

Jim and the two other officers led me to Court Number 3. It was bustling with people. Lots of black cloaks, black suits, some wearing white curly wigs accompanying worried-looking clients. I followed Jim to a half-empty bench in the middle of the room and sat down. To my relief I spotted Barry and Aaron sitting behind us. My eyes met Barry's and I almost burst into tears. He mouthed the words, 'You'll be OK,' before I faced forward again. We waited as, one by one, people's names were called. At one point I turned to Jim and quietly asked, 'Jim, why is this happening?' He replied, 'I don't know, Gail. I don't know.' God love him, I know he had a job to do but I got the impression that he didn't like doing this one.

After about an hour, my name was called. Curiously, there seemed to be confusion in the room. As it turned out, the clerk of the court was down in the cells looking for me. Everyone seemed concerned until Jim stood up and said, 'The prisoner is in the body of the court!' It was only then that I realised Jim had done me a huge favour by not sending me to the cells when we arrived at court. I thought to myself: what a decent man he is – he didn't have to do that, but he did.

I stood up and timidly walked towards the judge's bench. She had short blonde hair and a 'no nonsense' look upon her face. I stood there as muffled words were spoken, barely audible given all the noise in the room. The result of this short exchange was that I was now on unconditional bail and had a date to attend my next hearing. For now I was free to go.

When we left and were in the sanctuary of our own car, I cried all the way home.

10

Throughout all the madness of the previous few months, I had developed a very close friendship with Tom Curran. We now had so much in common, as well as a mutual understanding of the stresses involved in the subject at hand. While my garda interviews were taking place, I had legal representation, and their advice to me was to exercise my right to silence and always to say 'no comment' to the guards' questions. But I was not satisfied to remain silent. I had nothing to hide and I felt in my heart that Bernadette's story needed to be told with honesty, regardless of the implications for my own welfare. Tom often mentioned the name of a solicitor friend of his, Dara Robinson, who had offered his services should I require them. In my naivety at the time, I didn't think I would ever have to make that call but kept his name at the back of my mind just in case. On the day I received the call from Detective Jim Byrne informing me that I would be charged, Barry made a call to Tom asking if he could help in any way. Tom then rang Dara and arranged for us to get in touch to set up a meeting. It was scheduled for the day after my first appearance in court.

Dara's firm, Sheehan & Partners, had offices on Francis Street in Dublin. Barry and I arrived half an hour early and sat in our car going over everything we wanted to discuss. I was extremely nervous and became quite emotional again. When we entered the building, I remember standing in the lift not really knowing what to expect. We were greeted by a friendly receptionist, who directed us to a small waiting room.

About ten minutes later, a tall, slim and well-dressed man appeared at the door and introduced himself as Dara. We shook hands and followed him into his office. I have a thing about handshakes – I feel it says a lot about a person – and Dara's was firm and strong. First impressions are important and, although we had just met, I liked him already.

We sat and went over the entire story. The expression 'the devil is in the detail' was going around inside my head and if Dara Robinson was going to represent me I wanted him to know everything, no matter how insignificant some parts seemed. He wrote down all we said. It felt strangely safe to put my freedom, indeed my future, in the hands of this man. At no point in our conversation did he mince his words: quite the contrary, in fact. He explained that there was always a chance that at the end of our journey I might still go to prison for the role I had played in Bernadette's death. He never sugar-coated anything, which I respected. He added that because my case was the first of its kind in Ireland, there was no precedent to refer to. He also informed me that it would be a trial by jury.

The meeting eventually came to an end with Dara telling me to go home and do my best to relax, and that he would be in touch soon. On the drive home I asked Barry to go over all we had discussed. Even though I had concentrated as much as possible on everything Dara told us, I was so nervous that I forgot most of it. Once again Barry came to the rescue.

We had another meeting a couple of weeks later, in early 2014. I was due in court again and Dara wanted to tell us what would happen on the day and what he would be requesting. He always went over everything in great detail, which took away a lot of my fear.

Too much information is better than too little. It stops your imagination from running away with itself.

A few days later I was back in Court Number 3. It was packed to the doors once again with the usual cloaks, suits and clients. After a long wait, my name was called and I approached the bench. Dara requested that bail continue and that an assignment of free legal aid meet the cost of my defence. To our huge relief, both were granted. It was time to return home again, back to over-thinking, over-analysing and sleepless, stressful nights.

Our third meeting with Dara was predominantly to discuss choosing my legal team. On this day he was accompanied by a young woman called Aisling, from Northern Ireland, who was a qualified solicitor. We warmed to her immediately. Aisling's role was to assist Dara with the day-to-day preparation of my defence. He went into detail about whom he had in mind for my senior and junior counsel. To begin with, I was a little lost as I had never heard of these professions before. He said he had a top barrister in mind by the name of Diarmuid McGuinness for senior counsel. He joked about his bedside manner, but that he was a genius at what he did. I trusted Dara so I didn't argue with that. He then talked about my junior counsel and mentioned a lady called Anne Rowland. He said he was going to arrange for Barry and me to have a meeting with her.

Summer was around the corner and many weeks passed by with no news. It was a constant battle to just get through each day. In a way I wanted time to pass slowly because I was terrified of what the future might bring, but then again I wanted the whole mess over and done with no matter what the outcome because it was so exhausting to be worrying all the time. I also refused to burden anyone, especially my children, with the level of anxiety I was feeling, so I kept a lid on it all until Barry and I were alone. He always knew what to say and, when there were no words to help, he just held me in his arms. I don't think I would have survived if I didn't have him by my side, fighting my corner and keeping me both safe and sane.

Our meeting with Anne was finally arranged. I hoped I would like her. So far I wouldn't have changed anyone involved in my case and wanted this meeting to go the same way. Dara, Barry, and I sat in his office going through some paperwork while we waited for Anne to arrive. When she entered, she smiled at me warmly and shook my hand firmly. I thought to myself, 'We're off to a good start.' When she sat in front of me, we both noticed our matching lipstick and nail varnish and shared a giggle. She had a colleague with her whose name was Lorna. This young woman looked no older than twenty, and I learned that she was Anne's 'devil', a name given to a newly qualified barrister learning the ropes for a year by shadowing an experienced junior counsel. I knew after only a few short minutes of talking to her that Anne was the right person to be part of my legal team. She was professional and to the point, which was exactly what I wanted. I definitely had more hope in my heart leaving Dara's office that day.

Although, legally, matters were somewhat falling into place, things at home were becoming increasingly difficult. Days and nights were filled with almost constant conversations about the entire mess. We went over and over everything. Looking back, I realise how very important all this was but it also drained me of what little energy I had. During one of our talks, Barry suggested that I write it all down, everything that Bernadette and I had gone through from the beginning of our relationship all those years before and right up to the present day. It would be my version of events and the facts that might help keep me out of prison. I was so tired of it all that at the beginning I was reluctant to embark on putting it all on paper. The thoughts of having yet another thing to do, more energy used up, annoyed me but if I have learned anything in this life, it's that Barry is very wise. After a little resistance, I agreed to do it.

It was also important to write down the roles that others had played over the last months and weeks of Bernadette's life. I wasn't alone in helping her to shut down her life and make final arrangements, so this information was vital to paint a complete picture. I set about writing, paying particular attention to the time between the dates outlined in my charges, which were 10 March to 5 June 2011. It was only fair that if the judicial system was going to punish me for simply loving someone enough to give them help and support while they went through the hardest, most frightening thing anyone could have to face, then I wasn't going down without a fight.

Dara rang a week or so later to let us know that our first meeting with Diarmuid McGuinness SC had been arranged. I was nervously excited about meeting him. His office was in the Law Library on Church Street in the centre of town, and as we walked into the building, we spotted Lorna, Anne's understudy, standing in the lobby. It was lucky we'd met her when we did because she was able to tell us we were actually in the wrong place. It was just coincidental that she was there briefly on other business, so when she was finished she escorted us to the correct building. It wouldn't have been a good start to be late for Diarmuid on our first meeting.

We hurriedly made our way to where Anne and Dara were waiting, and then took the lift to the fifth floor and Diarmuid's office. Before I walked through his door, Anne took me by the hand and whispered, 'You are in the presence of greatness,' and threw me a reassuring smile. Diarmuid was sitting at his desk and stood to greet us all. One by one we shook hands and sat down. He oozed professionalism. I liked him and how he carried himself. We sat and went over all the details of the case. Mostly it was my team talking legal talk but I held my own as best I could. I noticed that Diarmuid occasionally chewed on the end of his pen, which conjured up memories of *Rumpole of the Bailey*, a programme I used to watch as a child. Once again I left a meeting feeling a little safer and a tiny bit more confident, knowing that I had exceptional people fighting my corner.

Soon afterwards I had another appearance at court, this time to receive the book of evidence. Fortunately, I was in and out in a relatively short time with only Dara, Barry and me needing to attend. Dara took whatever paperwork I was given back to his office to make copies for us and his team, and arranged a meeting for a day or two later so we could discuss the contents. There were lots of statements from garda officers, from Elizabeth, Bernadette's neighbour, from Bernard her nephew, from her sisters Catherine and Beatrice, and various others, including the funeral director and her solicitor.

As I read the statements, I couldn't believe what I was seeing. In Beatrice's statement she expressed her dislike for me and said that I had some kind of a hold over her sister – there were so many lies that it sent me into a state of panic. For months I had spent day and night consumed with worry and now, reading her statement, my fears were multiplied a hundredfold. I must have read her words twenty times or more, attempting to absorb it all. I'm sure there was a level of self-preservation in the statement but in writing what she had written she was tightening the already choking noose around my neck. It felt like I was being hung out to dry. I was devastated.

I began to read Mary Lundy's statement. In it she answered the guards' questions with a continual 'no comment'. I felt very much alone.

The only control I had was to go back to my writing and make sure every detail, no matter how small, was put down and explained. A week or so later I called to Dara's office to deliver what I had written, outlining things that no one else but Bernadette and I could have known about. He went through the pages, speed-reading them before saying, 'Well done. All this information can only do good.' I was really pleased with his reaction. Dara told me he would make copies of my document for everyone on my team.

Christmas 2014 was now only around the corner and Barry and I were determined to make it one to remember. I had terrifying images of having Christmas visits in whatever prison I might end up in, and imagined waving goodbye to my beautiful grandchildren as they left. These thoughts were some of the scariest in my mind but I knew it was better to prepare myself for this possibility than to run away from what might happen. We had a wonderful Christmas, surrounded by family and friends, counting our blessings and taking stock of just how fortunate we were in the great scheme of things.

New Year came and went in what felt like the blink of an eye and we were back to reality with a great big bang. Within a week or so I returned to court to enter my plea. When my name was called, I stood in front of the judge and, in as firm a voice as I could muster, said, 'Not guilty.' I felt so small standing in the courtroom, and I wondered how on earth I was going to manage when my actual trial started.

At home it was all that we talked about, but no matter how much we discussed it, it was impossible to draw any conclusions. Having no precedent to refer to made everything so much worse. My mind was constantly awash with scores of unanswerable questions. Would the powers that be go a little easier on me because I was the first to ever be prosecuted for this alleged crime, or were they going to throw the book at me in an attempt to make an example of me so as to deter anyone else from doing what I had done? At times I thought I was losing my mind.

Our family, friends and, most importantly, our children were always a great support. I would have been lost without their patience, love and distractions, but they too were showing signs of stress. My sister Linda was particularly affected. We are so close, and her inability to protect me as my big sister took a huge toll on her. When we talked, she would often break down in tears.

My next meeting with the team was short but significant. They had all read what I had written and we went over it all in great detail. I cannot explain how joyous I felt knowing that everyone in the room believed in me. Of late, I had been nearly suffocated by my fear of Bernadette's family and what they might say in court.

The day of my pre-trial, 13 March 2015, arrived. I didn't think my stress levels could get any worse but I found I was a bag of nerves. At an earlier meeting Dara had explained exactly what to expect. Today would be when both defence and prosecution confirmed whether or not they were ready to go ahead with the case. As always, just having Dara by my side made me feel so much safer. His air of confidence always reassured me and, although he never pretended to know how it would play out, I had total faith that he would do his very best for me.

Outside the court a few photographers had gathered and they took their usual shots of us heading into the building. I didn't really have to do anything in the courtroom, so I just stood there straining to hear what was being said. On the far side of the room were the prosecuting senior and junior counsel, Remy Farrell and James Dwyer. My trusty team were on the other side. Lorna had been replaced by a new devil called Lisa, as her year shadowing Anne had come to an end. As far as I could make out, all seemed in order, so proceedings ended rather quickly and it was home to play the agonising waiting game once again.

There were only four weeks left until my trial began on 13 April, bringing with it an entirely different type of preparation. The practicality of having suitable clothes to wear became an issue because my wardrobe consisted of only jeans and T-shirts. My stress had caused me to quit my taxi business, so I was broke. Barry's financial situation was not much better. He had missed many days at work because I was in too much of a mess to be left alone a lot of the time. To my delight, I was able to borrow suitable outfits from the women in my family, who put together for me two or three different skirts and tops. Barry and I borrowed money from family to pay bills that were now mounting up, and cash we would need to get through the three weeks of the trial. Looking back, I don't know how we would have managed without their help – they provided a life-line when we needed it most.

Another thing that greatly helped were the supportive letters (some of which reached me with nothing more written on the envelope than my name and 'Tallaght'), cards and flowers that arrived from strangers around the country. So many mornings I sat at my kitchen table in tears reading their beautiful and at times heartbreaking messages. Many people who had experienced the awful death of a loved one wrote that if they had had the opportunity to help to end their suffering, they would have done so. It was the strangest sensation, being faced with the possibility of being a convicted criminal and yet not feeling like one at all. The support of everyone made me feel so proud of who I was.

Over the next week we had a brief meeting with Dara and then one last meeting with the whole team. We went over everything with a fine-toothed comb. I was still terrified of Catherine and Beatrice and what they might say. Dara's words, 'Try to hold it together,' went around and around inside my head but I could feel myself weakening the closer I got to the big day.

Our final meeting lasted about an hour. Everything seemed to be in order: all boxes ticked, all questions asked; but behind all the reassurances I received, terror was rapidly growing inside me. The overwhelming urge to run away was again getting stronger. On the one hand, I wanted to sit into my car and just keep driving in a last-ditch attempt to shelter myself from the onslaught of questions and accusations I was about to face. But, on the other hand, I was determined to stand proud and strong. I had loved Bernadette with all my heart and the only thing I was guilty of was being a true and loyal friend. I had many things to fear but absolutely nothing to be ashamed of.

11

Despite the worries being generated by my upcoming trial, my family, friends and I all had practical things to take care of in advance of it. Three weeks is a long time if you have children for whom you have to arrange babysitters or if you require time off work, so everybody involved in supporting me was very busy. As already mentioned, Barry and I had borrowed a few bob from the family to help us get through the weeks ahead, especially for daily expenses while at court. Even at an emotional time like this, the mundane things of life have to be considered.

I had obtained as many outfits as I would require, making sure to have enough so that I wouldn't be seen wearing the same one two days in a row. Funny how the mind works but I wasn't sure yet if the media would be friends or foes, so eliminating this one little thing seemed important – and, besides, I wanted to look my best. I was determined to look respectable, and was also grateful to Dara and Anne, who gave me specific instructions relating to how much jewellery and makeup to wear. I have many piercings that I had to remove, and I made sure none of my tattoos were visible. There are those who judge a book by its cover and, in case there were some of these on the jury, I erred on the side of caution and kept my outfits as neutral as possible. Dara and Co. hadn't led me once in the wrong direction so far and it would have been foolish to ignore their advice now.

In the week running up to 13 April, neither Barry nor I got much sleep. If I thought I was consumed with worry before, it had definitely now gone up a few more notches. I was in and out of bed constantly during the night. Sometimes I went downstairs alone to have a good cry, and many other times Barry joined me in the kitchen and we would talk and talk. No matter what aspect of the case we discussed, it almost always ended with me saying, 'I wouldn't change a thing, and I have no regrets.' I hadn't at any point let down Bernadette or myself, and in life and in death I supported her and her choices. I had been honest with the authorities from the get-go and at no point did I ever think of turning back the clock to change anything. So here I was, up to my neck in hot water but without feeling any regrets. It was the strangest sensation; I would imagine that most people facing a possible fourteen years in prison would think differently, but not me. I felt proud of myself – terrified, but proud.

The week went by in the blink of an eye and the very early hours of Monday morning arrived. I woke at around 6 a.m. and lay in bed, barely able to hear the birds' morning chorus over the pounding of my heart. I didn't want to get up. I knew that once my feet hit the floor, that was the point of no return, and it scared the pants off me. But I knew there was nowhere to run. I simply had to do this and if the layers of fear were peeled away, what I felt was an enormous need for truth and justice.

I imagined what Bernadette would say if she was here: 'Make sure your jewellery matches', and then, 'Stand straight, chin up and go show the world what you're made of, girl!' So I dragged myself out of bed and had a hot, very sweet cup of tea to try to calm my nerves.

My daughter Dawn, my brother Steve, Barry and myself were travelling together. Barry was driving. My son Aaron and his partner Laura had to drop their daughter Baylee to a sitter and would meet us in the court. As we left the house, a few of our neighbours came over to offer words of good luck and much-needed hugs. The journey into the city was sombre, with very little said. As we approached the Criminal Courts of Justice building, we spotted a handful of photographers on top of the steps, so I ducked down in my seat to avoid being seen. Barry turned left on to Infirmary Road beside the courts and pulled in at the side of the road to let us out before heading off to find a parking spot. I stood in the warm sun shivering with tension as we waited for others to join us. My brother Paul and his partner Anna arrived first, followed shortly by my sister Linda, her husband Liam, Loren her daughter, Loren's boyfriend Stephen, and Angela, a friend of Linda's. Barry didn't take too long to find a parking space and joined the group for lots more hugs and kisses. Then we all took a collective deep breath and made our way down the hill to the waiting media. Barry and I were out in front, feeling strong and brave. As we turned the corner, the photographers jumped to attention and came rushing towards us. Click, click, click went their huge cameras. A voice in my head kept repeating, 'Head high, Gail, but not too high.'

Their clicking ceased as we walked through the glass double doors leading to the security desks and lobby. It was arranged that we would meet Dara outside

Court Number 7 at 9.45 a.m., but he was nowhere to be seen. We sat and waited anxiously on the cold marble benches, and I tried to reassure myself that he would arrive soon. I knew I would feel calmer once he was there. More people arrived: Aaron, Laura, my oldest brother Dave with his wife Sheila, and their daughter Roxy. Then I saw the beautiful reassuring face of my good friend Sinead. I also spotted Tom Curran, who gave me an enormous hug.

Tom told me that Philip Nitschke (aka Doctor Death), head of Exit International, the organisation from which Bernadette had sourced her information in order to achieve a dignified death, was somewhere in the building and was going to attend my trial. My heart began to race with panic. Oh God, I thought, what would Dara say? He's going to go ballistic. I'm in enough trouble as it is without the attention this man's presence could bring because Nitschke is quite a vocal man and nothing held him back. Before long, Dara arrived and I told him the news. His reply was calm and cool. He said, 'It's a free court but I'm going to have a word with him and tell him to keep his mouth shut!' God, I loved Dara. We continued chatting before I headed for the café and a final opportunity to talk and gather my thoughts.

When we returned to the court, I saw that Diarmuid, Anne and Lisa had arrived. There was lots of hustle and bustle and a few passers-by gave me a nod and a smile. I couldn't help feeling how strange it was to be recognised. I hadn't given any thought to anyone knowing who I was. As we entered the courtroom, I realised that it was a shared court, with many people coming and going. Diarmuid took me to one side and told me he was going to ask for my trial date to be put back, because of queries he had for the Director of Public Prosecutions. I was too distracted to absorb the reasons he gave and I can't recall what they were. He was successful and was granted an adjournment until the following Thursday. It felt like a tiny stay of execution but, on the other hand, the thought of having to wait three more days was hard to bear.

Before going home, my team asked Barry and me to stay behind for a brief meeting. Six of us crammed into a stiflingly hot, tiny room situated just outside the court, and went over details regarding one of my interviews, which had taken place in Rathmines Garda Station before Bernadette's death. Apparently, it had been suggested that I had said at some stage that if the authorities stopped Bernadette from going to Dignitas in Switzerland, her backup plan was to use Exit International. I froze in my chair when I heard these words. Where had this come from? Exit had never even been mentioned while Bernadette was making her Dignitas plans because she never thought these plans would have to be cancelled. Besides, I had never even heard of Exit before her travel arrangements were stopped. How was I going to prove that I hadn't said it? All I could do was hope that the truth would come out, helped along by my trusted legal team.

This information was apparently in some report, but it was nowhere in the interview memos. Surely to God if the gardaí had this information before Bernadette's death, it would have been sufficient reason to call on her. The ensuing meeting would have clarified everything straight from the horse's mouth, but no such meeting had ever been scheduled. Even more surprising, it was uncovered that there was nothing on Bernadette in the jobs book, an in-station log of all investigative jobs covered, until 11 August, nine whole weeks after her death. This clearly indicated that initially the authorities did not suspect foul play. Our meeting ended. The waiting media had lost interest and gone home. We walked to our car uninterrupted.

It would later transpire that no allegation of this sort was to be made at the trial – but at the time it was details like this that threw my mind into a spin for days, wondering what it meant, and what implications it could have.

That is a side-effect of being on trial – even when you are completely innocent. Unsure as to how anything will play out, you begin to second-guess everything. Small inconsistencies in a statement that may just be mistakes, or the particular use of language – these things seem more sinister, and your mind goes to town thinking what's behind them, what they might mean. Being on trial is like being in a constant state of high adrenaline. Your senses are heightened. You imagine that the smallest detail can create the biggest effect – and in truth you are not far wrong. Ultimately, it is your word against that of another person and it is easy to become unsure of who you can trust. It is like living in an altered reality, where anything is conceivable – even spending over a decade in a prison cell for something you did not do. The stress is so all-consuming that it is hard to ever relax, or truly let down your guard. My home was my sanctuary, but during those dark days, the outside world was anything but.

Thursday began with me lying in bed, once again staring at the ceiling and struggling to focus on anything. I showered and did my best to get some breakfast into my grumbling and anxious stomach. Today it was just Barry, me and the kids travelling to court together. It was nice for all four of us to be together, even for a little while, and it gave us time to make sure that each one of us was OK. I got a call from Barry's cousin Trish, who told me that she and her family had already arrived at the courthouse and would meet us in the café before it was time for me to face the music again. My brother Paul and Anna were due to meet us there too. It was so reassuring to know that we had such great support. We also knew that Linda, Liam, their son Ryan, Loren, Stephen and Angela were waiting for us on Infirmary Road. As we drove up the road, we saw that the eager photographers had sussed out our routine and were peeking around the corner on the lookout for us. Because of this, we decided to park higher up the hill just out of eyeshot. It was vital that we had at least five minutes to prepare ourselves. When we were ready, we took the short walk down past the photographers and through the courthouse doors, back once again into relative privacy.

While queuing for tea, I spotted Sean Fitzpatrick of Anglo-Irish Bank fame standing behind me. He clearly didn't have a clue who I was but I said hello anyway. We chatted briefly about our shared lack of sleep and wished each other good luck before parting ways. After many hugs from family and friends, Barry and I headed to Court 7. Dara was waiting and took us to one side. He told us that Diarmuid and Anne had tried to have count one of the three counts on my indictment dropped. (The three counts were: 1. attempting to purchase tickets to travel to Zurich, 2. sending the Western Union money order to Mexico to purchase the Nembutal, and 3. making Bernadette's funeral arrangements.) He explained that the DPP felt that because the travel arrangements for Zurich had been made within the Irish state, there were grounds to continue with the charge. About five minutes later, Diarmuid joined us and suggested a request to adjourn proceedings until Monday. I felt really frustrated. I just wanted the trial to begin so that it could end. To my relief, Dara intervened and between them they agreed to go ahead with the selection of the jury. I breathed a huge but nervous sigh of relief.

In the crammed courtroom three or four cases were to be heard before mine. When my turn came, the judge allotted us Court Number 12 and told us my judge was going to be Judge Pat McCartan. When I walked into the new court, my stomach somersaulted. Everything seemed all the more real now. I was guided to the dock by Dara, with Barry holding my hand as always. As I glanced around, I saw the many faces of my loved ones; they all looked so worried. There was a row of reporters sitting in front of them, and a lot of gardaí milling around. Barry leaned over and gave me a kiss before taking his seat. I sat back in the wooden box, my home for the next two and a half weeks. All I could do for now was sit there and observe. Diarmuid and Anne were going through paperwork and Dara walked around making sure everything was in order. Remy Farrell, the prosecuting senior counsel, was there along with his junior counsel James Dwyer.

Opposite me, and just behind where the jury were to sit, was a very large wooden door. I sat staring at it, waiting for it to open, every muscle in my body rigid with tension. Maybe Dara noticed my panic because he walked over to me and explained what was going to happen next regarding jury selection. He said that I would have some say in the choosing or not choosing of certain jurors, but I would have only seconds to decide. Judge McCartan then entered the room, so we all stood up. He was a slim man in his early sixties. There was an air of confidence about him; maybe all judges had this but I hadn't been in contact with many in my life so it stuck out for me. From 1987 to '92 he had been a TD for the Workers' Party; his constituency had been Dublin North-East.

On the table in front of the judge's bench was what could best be described as a raffle barrel, the type that spins, with a little door from where one would pull a raffle ticket. The court registrar spun it and took out one piece of paper at a time which had jurors' names and numbers written on them. She handed the papers to another woman who then left the room. Within minutes the big brown door opened and twenty people entered the room. I frantically glanced from face to face in an attempt to figure out who of the potential jurors looked reasonable and fair, but it was impossible to judge. Each of them glanced in my direction before walking to the witness stand where the Bible or the Koran was waiting to be sworn on. In Dara's hand was a list of their names and addresses and, for some of them, their occupations. He had limited information on them but enough to know whether we wanted them or not. Dara could and did challenge, without cause, approximately seven of the jurors. At Dara's requests some people were challenged and some were excused on the basis that they were unable to commit for one reason or another. One group after another entered the room until eventually all twelve jurors were selected. I couldn't help wondering what they were all thinking, these six men and six women in charge of my future.

As I looked around the room, Barry's eyes met mine, and he gave me a reassuring smile. I looked towards my beautiful daughter, who was already in tears, and then Aaron, who was being strong and proud as usual. They were only feet away from me but I still felt extremely unprotected and vulnerable. Diarmuid, who up to now had been very forward and confident in his demeanour, was quite low-key and reserved when addressing the judge. I presumed this was a show of respect for his authority. Before proceedings were called to an end for the day, both sides agreed to have out-of-court discussions relating to one or two upcoming issues. We were due back the next day, Friday, but Monday was when the trial was to begin officially. We left the building and the photographers chased us up the hill, running in front of us to get their perfect shots of two haggard and stressed-out people. All I kept thinking was, 'Why the hell did we not arrange a getaway driver to pick us up?' But we weren't to know because nothing like this had ever happened to us before and, besides, they would have still chased us even if we had a car waiting. It was a very uncomfortable feeling.

Friday, 17 April arrived and again I lay in bed fighting back tears of frustration and worry, made all the worse by a lack of any proper sleep. My appetite was at rock bottom, which made me feel even more drained, if that was possible. We made our now all-too-familiar journey to court where we ran the media gauntlet without too much fuss. It wasn't something I ever got used to but it became a little less daunting over time. In court there was a lot of back-and-forth arguing between counsel. Dara wasn't with us that day and I deeply missed his reassuring winks, nods and explanations. However, I was increasingly in awe of Diarmuid and Anne, observing what an amazing team they were. Once again they tried to have Count One of my indictments dropped, but sadly to no avail. We were all understandably disappointed. Remy Farrell was making submissions on a number of legal technicalities, while James Dwyer sat behind him studying his papers with a serious air and assisting his senior's arguments. Whenever he looked in my direction, I felt he was looking into my very soul.

At the end of much to-ing and fro-ing, it was decided that Counts One and Two were to be amended. Inwardly I prayed that evidence over the coming days would help. If I'm honest, I was more than a bit lost in it all but I trusted that my legal team had everything in hand for me. I had also come to the realisation that I liked the judge, and truly felt that his decisions were balanced and fair. He informed us that we had been allotted yet another courtroom, Court Number 17, which we would go to on the Monday. No cameras were waiting when we left the court. We returned home and I put Barry to bed because he was running a high temperature. Before long it was evident that he had come down with the flu. It wasn't surprising that, with all the stress, his immune system was weak. He too was overwhelmed and exhausted.

Over the weekend Barry's condition deteriorated and was made worse by a very bad bout of diverticulitis, which he had suffered with for a couple of years. Since it is a stress-related condition, I urged him to sleep as much as he could before Monday, when things would inevitably get a lot more stressful. I spent most of Sunday downstairs alone, because I really didn't want to burden Barry with my tears. A lesser person would have been sick of seeing me distressed by now. Barry got up about five in the afternoon and saw that I was upset, so we sat and talked and talked. I always felt better when we thrashed things out between us. Barry has a great way of putting everything into context, something my frazzled brain couldn't do on its own. A couple of hours later he looked at me and said, 'It's OK to be upset here, but when that window blind goes up, we put on a brave face and show the world that we are strong.'

We headed out for a drive, not having any real destination, more to get away from the four walls of the house. It was a good distraction and did manage to clear our minds a little. When we returned, Barry went back to his sick bed and I decided it was time to clean and organise my house in an effort to clear both my brain and the overflowing linen basket before the next day, when the trial would finally begin in earnest.

12

On Monday, 20 April our day began by meeting our friends, family and others on Infirmary Road. I was heartened to see that our crowd of supporters had grown significantly over the past week. My brother Steve suggested that it might be a good idea to approach the reporters at the end of the hill and request that they keep their distance. To our great surprise, they agreed.

As we walked into the lobby, I spotted Elizabeth, Bernadette's neighbour, on the other side of the hallway. I was unsure how to handle things. I was aware she was a witness for the prosecution and didn't know if I was allowed to talk to her. I wanted to go over and say hello, because I always considered her to be a friend. Bernadette and I often used to chat to Elizabeth and on several occasions she and I had sat in her apartment talking about Bernadette's plans for a dignified death. She respected Bernadette's choice. But in the back of my mind there was a nagging worry, because in my book of evidence there were what seemed to me to be two conflicting statements from Elizabeth. In the first she talked about witnessing the very close relationship that formed over time between Bernadette and me; but in the second, she asked that this observation be taken out. In my over-analysing mind, I saw that the statements could have different meanings. The first could imply that I would risk everything, including my freedom, to help Bernadette and maybe that was why she had asked for the sentence to be removed.

When your brain is constantly overthinking, it tends to favour the 'worst-case scenario'. This is usually because you never want to be blindsided by something you missed. In those few short moments when these thoughts were zooming around in my head, I realised that Elizabeth was walking towards us. She wrapped her arms around me, giving me a great big hug, and in that moment I threw away any irrational and panicked thoughts I had. We talked briefly. I could see the stress all over her face and she seemed to be shaking a little. The thought of having to take the stand was obviously upsetting her. We parted ways and I joined our group at the lift. Before we got in, a cameraman from RTÉ approached Steve. He explained that he and his fellow cameramen were a bit uncomfortable having to cover the story and that they all wanted us to know that we had their support. He also asked if Barry and I could walk ahead of the group, because it was the shot they were all looking for. If we agreed to this, they promised there would be no more chasing us and shoving cameras in our faces. Without hesitation we agreed and thanked him for his kind words. I felt huge relief, not about the camera situation, but that the media were on our side. I had worried endlessly that they would attempt to portray me as a bad person, but this short meeting had put those worries to bed.

We had tea in the café and then made our way to our new courtroom, Number 17, Anne and Diarmuid were there already and took us to one side. They started asking me questions about a file named Exhibit A.D.8, which is the brown folder Bernadette had left at her apartment for the gardaí. Apparently one of the investigating officers had stated that I had had it in my possession and handed it in during one of my interviews. This was not true. Bernadette had actually issued me with specific instructions that it was to be left on her black African chest, to be easily seen for when the guards entered her living room. It contained many answers to questions that would inevitably be asked after her death. Anne and Diarmuid looked bewildered and requested a fifteen-minute adjournment to investigate exactly what was going on.

At 10.45 a.m. court began. Our new courtroom was much bigger than the last ones. There were rows of seats, with signs saying 'Reserved' specifically for my family and friends, and there were two full rows for reporters. However, this meant that I was much farther away from Barry and I didn't like that. There was a lot of commotion in the room: people rushing, getting things ready, and so many reporters and gardaí around. I recognised quite a few from both groups. I couldn't help feeling as if I was in some television courtroom drama. It all felt surreal.

Ten minutes later Judge McCartan entered the room and we all rose. There was talking between both legal teams and the judge before he instructed the clerk of the court to bring in the jury. My stomach was in a knot. But before I had time to think any further, twelve strangers walked in and took their seats. My eyes went from one to the other, and I did my best to not let them see me looking at them. They were a mix of old and young, one or two I didn't really like the look of. One of the twelve had been selected to be the forewoman, and on first appearance I found her intimidating. She was in her late forties, seemed quite upper class, and was understandably very serious. The judge greeted all the jurors and outlined instructions for them. Then it was onto opening speeches, which began with Remy Farrell, who was followed by Diarmuid. Within twenty minutes it was time for the trial to start.

The first witness the prosecution called was 'The Mapper'. He was a member of An Garda Síochána and his role was to map out the location of the alleged offence. Second to be called was the forensic photographer. He provided pictures of Bernadette's apartment, both inside and out, as well as relevant items that had been found in her living room. Included was a photo of her small pedal bin containing the empty bottles of the barbiturate Nembutal, which she had drunk to end her life. A copy of the photos was passed around to the members of the jury. Diarmuid cleverly cross-examined to bring out that there was no way Bernadette could have put the empty bottles in the bin herself because the bin was out of her reach. Both these witnesses were on the stand for only a short while.

Next up was Elizabeth, who looked very worried. I was so nervous for both of us. First to question her was junior counsel James Dwyer and, to my relief, he didn't have too many questions to ask. After only a few short minutes he ended his questioning and Diarmuid stood to begin his. Elizabeth seemed to struggle to hear his questions, but when she answered she was precise and firm in her tone. She told the truth and I was relieved to hear that it greatly favoured me. She talked honestly and beautifully about Bernadette and my relationship with her. She was on the stand for only about fifteen minutes. I can't believe how consumed with fear I had been for so long over this beautiful lady, but how was I to know what she was going to say in court? My paranoid brain hadn't worked properly because of stress, and somehow I had convinced myself that Elizabeth would say things differently. The relief was immense.

As I sat alone, I felt extremely unsure of myself, and struggled to find a comfortable place to observe the proceedings. To be honest, I wasn't sure where to look. If I looked towards the jury, I was afraid of making eye contact because my natural reflex was to smile, and that's the last thing I wanted them to see me doing. Or should I look at the judge? Maybe he would think I was trying to influence him in some small way. The witnesses? I was terrified they would think I was trying to intimidate them. My friends and family? The 'smile' problem again. If I looked down, I might look guilty, and if I looked up, I might come across as confident and I was anything but. My head was wrecked. So, in the end, I opted to look towards my legal team, which felt like the safest bet.

The next witness to be called was Garda Andrew

Dermody, He was one of the first officers at the scene of Bernadette's death, and he also interviewed Barry and me at the beginning of the investigation. I had warmed to him from our first meeting. He was accompanied by another garda, who was apparently the exhibit 'go-getter', who was to bring anything requested to the witness stand.

Before Garda Dermody was questioned, it was decided that Bernadette's suicide message would be played for the court to hear. There was a palpable hush throughout the room as everyone waited. Although both Barry and I had previously heard the recording, it was heartbreaking to listen to it again. Silence fell as the crackly message began. I did my best to compose myself but couldn't hold back the tears. As I looked around the room, it was clear how upsetting the recording was for nearly everyone there. The crazy thing was, in amongst all the sadness and tears, I was so happy to hear Bernadette's beautiful soft voice again. I missed her terribly.

Once the tape ended, people dried their tears and proceedings resumed. The exhibits officer stood close to Garda Dermody and handed him requested items. Exhibit A.D.8, the brown folder, was shown and it was announced that it had in fact been left at Bernadette's apartment and not handed in by me as previously reported. Diarmuid asked Garda Dermody to take out each individual page and read aloud the contents to the court. It contained two handwritten letters from Bernadette detailing our relationship, as well as letters to and from Dignitas and all her copied medical reports. Because it was late in the afternoon, the judge soon called an end to proceedings for the day.

Before leaving to go home, Barry and I were taken aside by my legal team. They had to hand statements to us which had been written by certain members of Bernadette's family and which were part of full disclosure. As I began to read, I was horrified at what I saw. It turned out that Bernadette's sister Beatrice had made statements in which she claimed that she and her entire family were terrified of Barry and me. However, at a later stage Beatrice requested these statements to be retracted from the record. She must have panicked once she realised that these would be used in court. Seeing these statements also confirmed that I wasn't all that crazy for having doubts or concerns about Bernadette's family that almost smothered me for years before my trial. I understood her panic in wanting the statements omitted because I know the truth will always surface and now she didn't have a leg to stand on.

On Tuesday, 21 April I was up at 6.30 a.m. feeling cautiously positive. Bernadette's sisters were taking the stand on that day and I didn't know what was in store. We ran the usual media frenzy before entering the sanctuary of the building's lobby. Up ahead of us we spotted Bernadette's family going through the security scanners. My stomach flipped with nerves and again I began to panic. Barry sensed my fear and squeezed my hand to calm me down. Catherine, Catriona, Shane, Bernard and Beatrice made their way towards the left-hand side of the hall, away from the route we needed to take to court. I did my best to look strong as we passed them but I could feel my insides slowly turning to a trembling mush.

As always, the court crew gathered in the café for tea and a chat. Some of us headed out to the smoking area for a quick one before proceedings began. As I walked through the exit door I spotted Bernard, Beatrice's son, over to my right. What a sight for sore eyes he was. I know I have mentioned it before but he and his wife Jenny were my favourite people in Bernadette's family. Back in the day I used to sit for hours talking to them while visiting Bernadette's family in Sligo, eating Jenny's delicious pies for which she was famous. Bernard looked up and we smiled at each other and shared a few nervous words. Because I was with Elizabeth, I was unsure if I should be speaking to Bernard, so we just wished each other good luck before parting. This brief meeting left me feeling less stressed because I realised that they weren't all out to get me, and the friendship he and I had was still very much intact.

First up was Garda Dermody again. Once more

he was questioned on the brown folder and on discrepancies relating to the timing of his statements. It was a short round of questions and he was out of the witness box in a matter of minutes. While walking back towards his seat, our eyes met and he gave me a little smile. I smiled back and couldn't help but feel sorry for him. Next to be called was his partner whose name I can't remember. I watched his face as his name was called, and saw him take a huge intake of breath and puff out his cheeks before walking to the stand. He certainly looked nervous. I didn't blame him after witnessing the level of questioning Garda Dermody had received. He was mostly asked the same questions and was on the stand for only a matter of minutes before being excused.

Beatrice was up next. Above the noise in the room I could hear my heart thumping in my ears and my throat began to feel tight as my blood pressure rose. What on earth was she going to say? We had never really seen eye to eye. As she began, I swallowed hard and braced myself for the worst, but it didn't come. Beatrice admitted that she had found out only the previous day that her son Bernard had planned to travel to Zurich with Bernadette and me, which I would imagine took a little wind from her sails. Mostly, she said really nice things about me. I was in shock. Her time on the stand was fairly short but, regardless of the length of her testimony, Diarmuid managed to get hidden little truths about my relationship with her sister to rise to the surface without Beatrice even noticing how cunning he was – given Beatrice's attitude towards me, which was often just barely concealed hostility, this wasn't something she would give up easily in the normal course of things.

Next up was Catherine. When I had seen her earlier in the lobby, I was too afraid to look in her direction but now that I did, I saw the strain of it all on her face. Then I looked around and saw that Bernadette's niece Catriona and her husband Shane had entered the room and taken a seat on the far side, away from where I was sitting. Catriona and I met eyes and, to my great surprise, she smiled, not a big smile but a reassuring one with warmth behind it. This one small thing brought a little bit of comfort to my panicking brain.

As Catherine took the stand, she was visibly shaking and her voice was so weak, it was barely audible. As always, the prosecution was the first to question her. This took only a few minutes. When Diarmuid began asking her questions, she listened carefully but was a little uncertain at first. He asked about cash Bernadette had left her, and she replied that €8,000 had been left for her in an envelope in Bernadette's apartment and a cheque was sent to her home address in Roscommon for the sum of €35,000 the week before Bernadette died. Most of Diarmuid's questions relating to money came directly from the written account I had handed to my legal team many months before. I was so happy that Barry had suggested writing it all down because I saw it was information vital to the truth and it was paying off before my very eyes. Diarmuid next produced Bernadette's two handwritten letters in the brown folder. He asked Catherine to verify that the handwriting was indeed her sister's, including the signatures at the bottom of both letters. She confirmed that they were. He then showed her a copy of the signature on the FedEx form, and again she clarified that it was Bernadette's writing and not mine. Soon after that, Catherine was excused, which I imagine couldn't have come quickly enough for her.

Bernard was called to the stand next. As ever, he looked calm. He was truthful and honest in his answers and his testimony backed up everything I had said. He was so humble and sincere and, as he made the short walk back from the witness box, he gave me a nod and a smile. I actually felt like pinching myself because so far all the prosecution witnesses had done me no harm. It left me feeling more than a little discombobulated. I honestly thought by now that at least one of them would have attempted to dent the truth, but no – so far, so good. Mind you, there was a long way to go. Last to be called for the day was the doctor who had pronounced Bernadette to be dead. Doctor Hooper also labelled relevant items found around her home. It wasn't long before he was excused.

Wednesday, 22 April began positively. Over the previous few days a few people had posted me messages of support and on this day I received many more beautiful handwritten letters and cards. I doubt the senders would ever realise or understand exactly how their words made me feel on these darkest of mornings. I was so grateful to each one of them for taking the time to send me messages of support. This feeling of warmth continued while I stood on Infirmary Road, for I was approached by well-wishers offering support and sympathy. These simple acts of kindness filled me with the reassurance that, even if at the end of this horrific journey I was found to be guilty, at least I knew that a lot of people had understood why I had done what I had done.

Before going into court, we were once again taken to one side and informed that Bernadette's solicitor, Maurice O'Callaghan, who was due to take the stand today, had told both legal teams that he had a professional duty of confidentiality to his client, Bernadette. He would not be able to give evidence unless the judge ruled that it was in the interests of justice to do so. According to my team, this was in my favour.

The day's first witness for the prosecution was

Caroline Lynch. She was the young woman I had dealt with in Rathgar Travel while attempting to buy the tickets for Zurich. She stuck to the facts and was excused within fifteen minutes. Following her was her boss, James Malone. He said that by informing the gardaí of Bernadette's intentions, he was protecting himself and his business. During questioning, it transpired that he had not printed off the travel tickets because he had made up his mind that Bernadette's plans would be cancelled. Diarmuid gave him very little breathing space between questions. He asked James Malone about a disabled person's right to travel. The owner of Rathgar Travel said that he was unaware that a disabled person was travelling.

Next up was the man who worked in the post office in Donnybrook. This was where I had posted the Western Union money order form to Mexico. By coincidence his name was Miguel. He repeated the few words he had said in his statement, nothing more and nothing less. Then came the delivery driver from FedEx. In his statement he had said that when he had entered Bernadette's apartment to deliver the package from Mexico, it was I who signed for it. I knew that wasn't true because Bernadette had signed for the package, knowing that the least interaction I had with this process, the safer I would be in the long run. However, for almost two years now it had been my word against his, since the only other witness was not available to confirm the details of the transaction. One of the charges against me was that I had signed for the package. As the Fed-Ex employee passed me in the dock, I remembered him well. He had stuck in my mind because he had come across as extremely bubbly and friendly when we had been in Bernadette's apartment. Now he looked nervous but he gave me a little smile before taking his seat in the witness box.

When Diarmuid asked him who had signed for the package he repeated what he had said in his statement. Diarmuid then handed him a copy on paper of the signature from the electronic keypad and in as loud and clear a voice as possible he said, 'Oh, oh. I must have made a mistake.' He seemed to be nearly as relieved saying these words as I was hearing them. I was thrilled, but knew I had to remain composed. At long last the truth was out. As he passed me to leave, the delivery driver gave me a smile and almost skipped from the court.

There was a brief pause in proceedings before Sergeant Sheeran from Rathmines Garda Station was called. I was fearful of his testimony, expecting it would be a negative account of things. He was one of the gardaí who had met me outside Rathgar Travel on that fateful day. But once again it transpired that I had no need to worry because everything Sergeant Sheeran said was positive. He told the court that I was one hundred per cent cooperative from beginning to end. I was starting to question exactly what was going on, because I felt as though I had been transported to some sort of parallel universe. So far, it seemed that all the prosecution witnesses could actually have been giving testimony for the defence. The picture being painted by all their accounts wasn't what I had expected at all. Not one negative word had so far been said about me. It was beyond anything I could have imagined.

Mary Cunniffe was next on the stand. She was the funeral director who had put all Bernadette's wishes into place. Earlier that morning we had met in the café and she threw her arms around me, almost squeezing the breath out of me with the hug. She wished me well and told me how nervous she was. Mary was full of reassurances for me. As she took the stand, I noticed how glamorous she looked, wearing a beautiful, beaming smile. When questioned, she confirmed all the facts as I had laid them out. She explained that when we were talking on the phone to make the arrangements, it had been a three-way call, with Bernadette's phone on loudspeaker. When asked if it was unusual for someone to make their own funeral plans, she explained that many people like to take charge of this themselves while they are still in a position to do so. Mary Cunniffe was a truly wonderful witness and, as she passed me, she gave me a warm smile. She now joined the ever-growing list of people who seemed to want me out of trouble.

There was a short appearance by the forensic computer analyst. He came across as very thorough, expert and by the book. He was the person who had unencrypted the Hushmail messages sent between Bernadette and Dorian Galeazzi in Mexico. Both sides had very few questions for him and he was soon back off the stand. Maurice O'Callaghan, Bernadette's solicitor, was the next to be called. Judge McCartan had ruled that it was indeed in the interests of justice for Maurice to give his evidence. He was dressed impeccably, wearing a dark three-piece suit, and had a natural air of confidence.

When his name was called there was some small commotion from the jury side of the room and it transpired that the forewoman brought to light the fact that she personally knew Maurice's wife which may have been a serious issue for me in the decision-making. The jury were excused temporarily while both prosecution and defence decided whether she could remain part of the jury. After a short conversation it was agreed that both sides had no objection to her continuing her role as a forewoman. The jury returned to their seats.

Maurice O'Callaghan confirmed that Bernadette was a strong lady. He talked about the level of detail he had gone into when ensuring that she understood the implications of leaving money in her will to a non-family member, something I learned about long after she had put these financial plans in place with him in the privacy of her home some months earlier. He had taken notes at all their meetings relating to the relationship she and I shared and was conscientious enough to have brought them to court. He read from them, quoting that Bernadette wanted to leave money to the people who had made her life better and how I had cared for her in ways no other friend could have. Maurice O'Callaghan was the best witness so far and cleared up any doubts people may have had about me and my intentions.

When both prosecution and defence had finished their questioning, Judge McCartan addressed Maurice with a question: 'Mr O'Callaghan, one of the charges against Ms O'Rorke is assisting a suicide by making funeral arrangements. Did you ever worry that, by taking instructions from Ms Forde relating to the arrangements in relation to her cremation and ashes, that you might have been assisting a suicide or breaking any law?' For a brief moment Maurice looked surprised at the question, but then replied firmly, 'No. As far as I was concerned, I was acting in a professional way and I do not consider anything I was doing for my client could be seen as breaking the law.' The judge replied, 'I agree with you,' then added, 'So the jury are being asked what is the difference between you, the professional, and Gail O'Rorke, the accused?'

These words seemed to hang in the air of that courtroom, floating around and being absorbed by everyone who had heard them. It was as if time had temporarily stood still and, while everyone was still processing the gravity of the last few moments, Judge McCartan said, 'Mr O'Callaghan, you are excused.' Jaws were hanging open around the room. This one simple but poignant question had left everyone flabbergasted. As Maurice passed me, he glanced over in a friendly way, which I was surprised at because I thought he was quite upset with me for having him there in the first place. I was not at all confident at this point in the trial because there was still so much to come, but I simply could not ignore the good things that were unfolding. Mind you, I knew that could all change in the blink of an eye because the rather scary Sean Campbell, Chief Investigating Detective Inspector, was next on the stand. To say that I was dreading this was an understatement. He was always the stern garda and I was convinced he was going to go hell for leather. He began by reading aloud excerpts from my statements. Junior counsel for the prosecution then took over the reading, but when he was only halfway through, Judge McCartan stood, calling an end to the day's proceedings. I was relieved but a little disappointed. I would have preferred it if this particular line of questioning had been put to bed, but for the most part I felt that the day had gone as well as I could have imagined.

I headed with family and friends to the smoking area for a talk before facing the ever-growing media who were waiting outside. We were not there long when Dara appeared, pointed directly at me and said, 'You, and only you,' before disappearing back through the door. I followed him, having to jog to keep up with him because he was walking so fast. He told me that the judge wanted to see me. I started to panic, but Dara said that maybe it was something to do with Count Three being dropped. Fingers crossed he was right. As we hurriedly entered the court, I saw Judge McCartan sitting behind his bench. He was holding a small piece of white paper, and when he turned it around we saw that written on it were the words 'Not Guilty' in big, bold block letters. What the hell? He told us that one of the jurors had found it in between the pages of his or her notepad and was extremely annoyed. My mind raced with fear. Where in God's name had it come from? It was confirmed that the courtroom was securely locked throughout lunchtime and would normally be empty but on this particular day the exhibits officer had stayed in the room and was able to verify that no one else had been there. It was also brought to light that these notepads were used and reused from case to case with the used pages being removed before each new trial began.

Eventually, to my enormous relief, it was confirmed by Judge McCartan that the piece of paper in question must have accidentally been left in the notepad from a previous trial. The judge, with a rare smile, said, 'Realistically, it is something the prosecution should worry about more than the defence.' He then walked from the room, leaving me in a mild state of shock. When I returned to my group of supporters, it was cause for much relieved laughter.

Thursday, 23 April. On Infirmary Road our court crew had grown even bigger. God bless each and every one of them for the sacrifices they had made to be there to support us. I know I have said this before, but we simply would not have got through this ordeal without them. I knew that Inspector Campbell would be back on the stand to conclude his testimony. The previous day had brought no bad news, so I naturally anticipated it would come today.

It began with junior counsel James Dwyer continuing from where he had left off. It took no longer than twenty minutes. It was then Diarmuid's turn to question Sean Campbell. Amazingly, the detective said absolutely nothing negative about me. He was professional, blunt and factual but, all in all, he portrayed me as an extremely cooperative and willing suspect. He even went so far as to say that I had helped greatly throughout the investigation. Diarmuid kept him on the stand for quite some time and I was aware that I was beginning to see Sean Campbell the 'human' rather than Sean Campbell the terrifying detective inspector with the cold, penetrating stare. I began to feel my tense and knotted muscles relaxing a little. Right now I wished I could be elsewhere in the courtroom, to not be the accused, so I could appreciate all the more the genius of my defence team. The current distraction of fear prevented me from truly seeing it in all its greatness. Diarmuid was in a league of his own, aided by Anne, who constantly went through pages and pages of legal volumes and handed him various sheets of paper with information or references written on them. When she wasn't doing this, she was whispering things in Diarmuid's ear. They worked beautifully together.

After Inspector Campbell had stood down, he was replaced by Detective Sinead O'Connor. When we had first met a few years before I liked her straight away. During my questioning at Donnybrook Garda station there had been a fifteen-minute break and she had sat and chatted to me. But she was here now to do her job and, as yet, I didn't know what to expect. Still, her time in the witness box was short-lived owing to the fact that, at the time of my interviews, Detective Jim Byrne had done most of the questioning. We shared a hint of a smile as Sinead O'Connor walked back to her seat and I couldn't help but wonder what the jury were thinking as they watched almost all the prosecution witnesses smiling at me. These were ostensibly the people against me, but so far the friendliness and respect between us was hard to hide.

The final witness for the day was the forensic computer guy again. His demeanour was standoffish and he came across as quite by-the-book. He painstakingly went through technical details relating to Bernadette's Hushmail account, reading aloud the correspondences between her and Dorian Galezzi. During his testimony, Judge McCartan broke the tension in the room when he put his hand in the air, calling a stop to the proceedings. He pointed at my sister-in-law Anna and said, 'You there, put your knitting away. Where do you think you are? You are in a court of law, not at the base of a guillotine.' Anna slowly sank down in her chair, mortified, and put her wool and needles back into her bag. Court began again. The witness wasn't on the stand for long. I was sure he was not that pleased to be asked to take the stand for the second time that week.

Judge McCartan excused the jury for the day but the rest of the courtroom remained seated to listen to legal arguments between the two teams. Diarmuid spoke at length about why he felt that all three counts on my indictment should be dropped. Anne continued passing him notes. Aisling, my second solicitor, remained her composed self and Dara continued to be my steadfast calmer of nerves. The judge also listened to all that was being discussed before calling an end to the day.

I couldn't wait to get home. I was tired, drained and emotionally exhausted. I was so looking forward to closing my front door, pulling down the blinds and drowning myself in the distraction of *Eastenders*.

13

Every morning I woke up feeling a little more nervous and afraid than the day before. The three weeks set aside for my trial were both dragging along but also zooming by and today, 24 April, we would find out if the judge had come to any decision about the three counts on my indictment. Once again I had the loveliest distraction in the form of more cards and letters from well-wishers, and I read them while sipping my morning cup of tea. I was comforted by the number of people who said that if they found themselves in my position, they would have done the very same thing. There were a couple of letters from people who had lost loved ones and whose deaths were devastating for those involved. They spoke of deep regrets they had about not discovering the options Bernadette had found. Among the many cards was one from a lady who wrote that she was not judging me for my actions, but that God himself might, and that I should take the opportunity to repent. We clearly believed in a very different type of God because I believed in the core of my soul that I had nothing to repent for. But her opinion was as welcome as all the others, because wouldn't it be a boring old world if we all thought the same way?

We arrived at court with enough time to grab a bite of breakfast in the café. I now had so many people with me that we took up most of the tables and chairs. Sitting in the corner were two men and one woman, all in their mid- to late sixties. I had seen them sitting at the back of the courtroom for the past week or so. As we stood to leave one of the men approached me and shook my hand. He offered us his sincere support, and went on to explain that his small group were all retired and liked to spend their days sitting in on different trials to observe the goings-on. It was a pastime they all shared. The rest of his group then joined us for a quick chat before we left the room.

While walking back towards the court, Barry and I spotted Inspector Campbell and a female garda sitting at a high table near the elevators. Earlier in the week Barry had had a small run-in with her when he had asked her to be quiet in court. She had barked an answer back at him before turning away. As we passed them, we said hello and to our huge surprise Campbell announced that they were all hoping for the same outcome, and his colleague smiled and agreed with him. I can't explain the relief I felt. Yes, I was still in a lot of trouble but my faith in humanity had just strengthened significantly. As we walked away hand in hand, Barry squeezed mine a little tighter in silent recognition of what had just happened.

The judge arrived in court to give his decision on whether the trial would proceed on the three counts against me. This had to be done in the absence of the jury, so he excused them before doing so. Then he addressed the first count: booking the travel tickets to Dignitas in Switzerland. In his delivery he was informative, fair and very by the book, but he concluded that count one would remain. Count two concerned my ordering the barbiturate Nembutal for Bernadette. The judge said he felt that there was simply not enough evidence to support the claim. He also felt that the jury would be forced to make a decision on something that he himself could not say was an offence. I could no longer hide my emotions and began to cry. I could also hear the emotional reaction from my family and friends but I dared not look in their direction because I was barely holding it together.

Then on to count three: the making of Bernadette's funeral arrangements. After a couple of minutes explaining the legal ins and outs, the judge once again concluded that this charge should also be dismissed. The testimony of Maurice O'Callaghan had probably helped him to come to this decision. By now many in the room had broken down in tears and I was a complete mess. As I cautiously glanced around the room, I saw that one or two members of the gardaí and a couple of media reporters were crying. Seconds after the judge walked from the room, I was swamped with hugs from everyone. I myself was in a state of disbelief and shock.

Next it was time for a little lunch and a lot of talk. Most of us were still crying but we did not lose sight of the one count still standing, which on its own was enough to send me to prison. On our way to the café, we bumped into Dara, who informed us that RTÉ had mistakenly reported on the radio that I had been acquitted of all three charges. He was furious but he assured me that the station would quickly rectify the mistake. Dara explained that it may be best not to call any witnesses in my defence, even though Bernadette's neurology specialist, Professor

Michael Hutchinson, and her multiple sclerosis nurse, Marguerite Duggan, were in the building waiting to be called. My stomach sank. I didn't really know how to feel about this decision. I knew that the twenty-one witnesses for the prosecution, in a very strange turn of events, had done me no harm; quite the contrary, they helped me beyond all my wildest imaginings, but surely to God my witnesses could only have made things even better. Marguerite and I had always got along so well during Bernadette's many hospital visits and I knew her testimony would have helped a lot. However, I was aware that Dara and his associates had not once pointed me in the wrong direction, so I gave no argument and agreed to his recommendations. He briefly explained what would happen should I win or lose my case, adding some advice on how to handle the media.

Back to court and to my imposing, uncomfortable little box. The judge was back in, as was the jury. After two whole weeks of looking at these twelve people, I was a tiny bit more comfortable about making eye contact. There were some whose eyes I still avoided, an elderly gentleman in particular. He was in his late sixties and since seeing him the first time, for some reason deep down in my gut I felt he judged my actions more severely than the others. It was just a feeling though. I wondered if the older jurors were more religious and less open to the subject of assisted suicide, or suicide on any level. I also wondered if the younger jurors had ever lost anyone close to them in a fashion that would have opened their minds to the desire to die with dignity. If only I could have read their minds. The forewoman, whom I was daunted by initially, had grown on me, and earlier I thought I had caught a slight smile from her upon hearing that two of my three charges had been dismissed.

Everyone in the room took their seats and the now familiar tense hush settled in the air. It was time for senior counsels' closing speeches. As always, Remy Farrell went first. He may have been my opposition but I have to admit he was good at his job. He covered many of the items that had been discussed in the trial, but while doing so implied a lot too. When talking about me, he complimented my good character. All in all he talked for about fifteen minutes. When concluding, he turned to the jury, looking from one to the other, and in his firmest voice yet instructed them to find me guilty. It was a truly impressive speech and one that left my insides quivering.

Then it was Diarmuid's turn. He stood facing the jury with his broad back to me, one knee resting on his seat. Taking a few seconds to compose himself after Remy Farrell's address to the court, he began by explaining how long his speech would take and should any member of the jury need a break then that was OK. Judge McCartan spoke up and said, 'I need a break.' The tension in the courtroom was broken and everyone laughed. Proceedings were then postponed for lunch.

When we returned to court, Diarmuid began once more. I simply cannot put into words what unfolded as he spoke. He was amazing to listen to, and I kept thinking to myself how lucky I was that he wasn't prosecuting me. He talked for forty minutes, with the entire room hanging on his every word. Occasionally he paused to gather his words. He took his glasses on and off intermittently, which only added to his impression of professionalism. I was sure in another time and another place he would have received a standing ovation when he had finished his speech. Today, when he concluded, Judge McCartan addressed the jury with instructions on what to do or not to do when they returned home for the weekend. The judge was to give his own address on the Monday morning but for now we would be agonisingly thrown into limbo.

The evening passed in a haze of consuming numbness. There were so many things to discuss, but for the moment neither Barry nor I had the energy to talk. It had been an unbelievably gruelling week with very little sleep, and again sleep evaded me as I tossed and turned all Friday night, drifting in and out of tormenting dreams. Saturday morning brought with it a much-needed lie-in. I got up around ten, so grateful that I was dressing in my casual wear of

T-shirt, jeans and boots. We did simple things like food shopping and visiting our beautiful grandchildren. They were the best distraction in the world and left no room for self-pity, with their abundance of energy and positivity. Samia with her softness and Baylee with her complete disregard for all authority were a blessing to my eyes and ears. Saturday was my brother Steve and his wife Ann-Marie's wedding anniversary, so we all headed to the nearby Kiltipper pub for a few drinks to celebrate their seven years together. We were all determined to put our stresses to one side and focus on having some fun, but inevitably conversations led back to the events of the past week. Then someone in our group asked the DJ to play a request for me. It was Queen's 'I Want To Break Free'. I was not one bit surprised, knowing my family's sense of humour. When the song ended, they all chanted my name while I sat there praying that the floor would open up and swallow me. We had a great night and did not go our separate ways until one in the morning.

When I woke on Sunday morning I made a conscious effort to get up and have as productive and positive a day as possible. Over the previous few weeks housework had been hard to face at the end of each day and the mess in the house was beginning to irritate me. They say a tidy home is a tidy mind, and so I cleared and cleaned as much as I could, welcoming the temporary distraction. In the afternoon Barry and I headed to The Old Mill pub for a carvery lunch. Several people recognised us from newspapers and the television; some just stared, while others came to offer their support. To be in such trouble and yet have so many well-wishers never ceased to amaze me.

When we got back home, we had a couple of visits from family and friends before I locked the front door and had a long soak in a hot bath. Ironically, it was Bernadette's old bath – the one she had to replace when she was no longer able to get in or out of it, even with the help of an electronic lift. I lay in it until the water was cold, before snuggling up with Barry on the couch. We were both very aware that it might be the last time for the foreseeable future that we had the freedom to do this. He held me in his arms for a long time, neither of us speaking. It was nearly 1 a.m. by the time we went to bed, and I remember thinking to myself, *Monday has officially arrived; only hours left before this nightmare comes to an end one way or another.*

I woke at 5 a.m., thinking about a bizarre dream I had during the night, that Barry and I had a huge argument over curling my hair before court. Eventually I got up at 6.45 a.m. I was more nervous than ever but deep, deep down I felt a strange glimmer of hope. I had no idea why. Maybe it was a subconscious coping mechanism that was giving me the fuel to get my day started, but it was there all the same. In amongst the post I found a handwritten letter from the RTÉ presenter Miriam O'Callaghan. It was beautifully written and brought to my eyes the first tears of the day.

The two of us readied ourselves for the arduous day ahead and travelled together to court. I was so happy it was just us because my brain had no room left to listen to anyone else. Seeing the sizeable group of eager cameramen and photographers waiting in their usual spot outside the court, I ducked down in my seat as we passed. We drove up Infirmary Road and I saw the largest group yet of family and friends. We chatted briefly and then, with Barry's hand firmly in mine, we approached the waiting media. I actually had grown to see them more as friends than as enemies. Throughout the whole trial they had been so supportive and honest in their reporting, and besides, they were all only trying to earn a wage like everyone else.

We all headed to the café for a cup of tea, where two of my mother's sisters, Joan and Hazel, were waiting to meet me. I was delighted to see them. They are tiny in stature but were huge in support, and they shared with me their frustrations about the trial before accompanying us into court. Before proceedings officially began, both counsels were asked if they had any questions they would like to ask. Diarmuid announced that he had a few. He explained to the judge that he felt he hadn't been given enough time to talk about my actions being purely preparatory, actions to plan something that had never taken place. He also asked for permission to read a passage from a book to the jury. The judge denied both his requests and I could see Diarmuid found it hard to hide his frustration.

It was time for the judge to give his own final address to the court before charging the jury to deliberate. Once again, he was thorough, fair and informative. I could see that he was being as 'human' as he could be but he didn't lean in either direction. When Judge McCartan finished talking he instructed the jury to go away and decide my fate. Before they left, he reminded them that a unanimous verdict was required. One by one they gathered up their paperwork and belongings and disappeared through the door to the room where my future would be decided. All we could do now was wait.

We all separated into smaller groups, some getting fresh air, others having a much-needed cigarette, some of us grabbing a bite to eat. I can honestly say that right then was the most worried I had felt throughout the trial. None of us really knew what to be doing with ourselves, and my mind constantly wandered to the jury in their room. Over the last few days, as my level of discomfort at having to sit face to face with the jury eased a little, I had unsuccessfully tried to read their body language. In the end I came to the conclusion that only God knew the outcome so I handed it over to my many angels and asked them to guide the jurors' decision-making.

My thoughts were interrupted when Dara came to tell us that we had been called back into court. When we were all seated, including the judge, the court clerk brought the jurors back into the room. To my disappointment and also relief, they were still undecided. They requested more copies of both my statements and of Exhibit A.D.8, the brown folder. They also wanted the term 'to aid and abet' to be explained in greater detail, and finally, that the term 'proximity of time', used several times throughout my trial, should be explained. I couldn't help but respect the level of attention they were giving to their roles. Then Judge McCartan asked Diarmuid for the very passage from the book he initially had denied him. McCartan read the words aloud and was asked by the jury to read it again. They were conscientious jurors but all I could think was, 'For the love of God, please just set me free!' Once again they left to deliberate but at lunchtime we were all back in court so the jury could be excused to go to lunch. It would be a torturous hour knowing that no decisions were being worked on.

The court crew were beginning to show cracks in their armour, and I could see the strain on many of their faces. I was still getting lots of smiles but the 'no result yet' was beginning to erode everyone's positivity. At 2 p.m. we returned to court, so the jury could officially be instructed to begin deliberating again. The forewoman was now my favourite of the twelve. She gave me a slight smile when entering court and again in Barry's direction as she left. So we all traipsed to the smoking area again where we had already spent endless hours pondering over each day's events. The only way to describe this wait is 'pure agony'. Surely to God it wouldn't take much longer. I was growing increasingly agitated being so far away from the courtroom, and since I felt I needed to be there when something happened, we made our way back up, taking our place on the long, cold marble benches outside.

It got to 2.30 p.m., 3 p.m. and 3.30 p.m., and on and on. Pockets of our supporters took turns gathering around Barry, me and the kids. Still no news and then at 3.55 p.m. word finally arrived that we were to go back into the courtroom. We all piled in and took our seats. As the jurors sat down, I noticed how stressed and tired some of them seemed. They also looked as though they had been arguing. The forewoman looked particularly fed up. The court clerk stood and asked, 'Have you, the jury, reached a decision?' The forewoman almost barked her answer, 'No!' The entire room exhaled the breath they were holding.

By now every single muscle in my body was rigid with tension, and once again the breathlessness of panic crept up inside me. I was devastated and thrown into a new level of worry, which I didn't think was possible. How was I going to get through another night of this? Judge McCartan gave the jury instructions about not discussing matters with anyone before excusing them and calling an end to the day's proceedings.

Before leaving for the day, Barry and I had a quick meeting with my legal team. They were in disbelief that no verdict had been reached and did their best to reassure me. They explained that the judge might direct a majority verdict either first thing in the morning or at midday when deliberations would have reached a total of five hours. Jokingly, Diarmuid said that if the jury found me guilty on a majority verdict, he himself was going to go to Dignitas. Our laughter to this inappropriate comment broke the tension and I confirmed that it wouldn't be me who'd bring him. We returned to the stressed-out crowd of supporters who were waiting to hear if we had anything of interest to tell them.

As we made our way towards the exit doors, Dawn said, 'Mam, there are a lot of photographers waiting outside.' As I peeped out from behind Barry's shoulder, I saw a wall of reporters all positioned facing the door, cameras at the ready, waiting to catch that one shot that would show the strain on our faces. All I wanted to do was stay inside and hide until they lost interest, but there was fat chance of that happening. We walked out and they got their shot but, to my relief, they didn't follow us. I looked around and saw that there were lots of people standing on street corners and footpaths outside. We really must have been some sight, so many of us marching united down the steps. I couldn't have felt alone if I'd tried. We turned left onto Infirmary Road and began making our way up the hill. I realised I was emotionally overwhelmed – I simply couldn't cope any more. I made a beeline for the other side of the road, hoping my loved ones would understand. Before long Barry and I were alone in the sanctuary of his car, but only after a lady whose house we'd parked outside offered sincere words of support. She was accompanied by a little boy, no older than five, who was obliviously munching on a bread and butter sandwich.

The drive back to our house was quiet. As always, Barry took care of me like no one else could. At home, after a cup of tea, I protested half-heartedly when he insisted I should take a nap. Surprisingly, sleep found me and I drifted off into beautiful blackness, uninterrupted by my usual distressing dreams. Two hours later I was woken by Barry's smiling face, another cuppa and as many hugs as I required. His practical philosophy reassured me – it was only another twenty-four hours, and we were well able for this. One more day wouldn't break us.

On Tuesday, 28 April I was awake before the birds' singing began and watched the light from the rising sun slowly creep across the walls of my room. I didn't want to get up, I didn't want to get dressed, and I didn't want to face the day. I lay there talking to Bernadette in my head, asking her to send me some strength to cope with what lay ahead. I really hoped that she could hear my pleas. I trusted she would: if anyone could, she could. I know it must have been killing her looking down and knowing we were going through this. I also felt that her perfect soul could see the bigger picture better than us mere mortals, and that whether this day brought good or bad news, there was a reason for it all. I finished by telling her that I loved and missed her, before dragging myself from the safety of my bed. I showered and unsuccessfully attempted to eat some toast. I was on the verge of throwing up, with the level of anxiety I was feeling. Barry wasn't much better. We travelled, just the two of us, in almost complete silence. What was there to say that hadn't been said a thousand times already? I asked God to please let this end today one way or another because the emotional cracks were widening and we were on the verge of falling in.

There must have been thirty or more people waiting to meet us at our usual 'pre-court' hangout on the hill, and when we walked down and around the corner, photographers ran at us from all directions. Then we made our way into court for 10.30 a.m. where Judge McCartan instructed the frazzled jury to return a majority verdict. Time to play the painful waiting game once again. We splintered into smaller groups in an attempt to both support and distract one another. Nerves had got the better of us all, to the point where occasionally there were bursts of nervous giggles. We took turns going for tea and nicotine breaks. They even managed to drag me away from the courtroom door once or twice but I couldn't get back to it quick enough. Tick tock, tick tock.

Occasionally the court door opened as someone left, and every time it did we all jumped, thinking the verdict was in. Tom Curran was struggling to cope and had become very upset. My heart broke for him as he had already been through so much with Marie. Time crawled by until lunchtime when everyone was called into court so the jury could be told to go for lunch. For them it was a much-needed break, but for me it was another hour for my life and future to be on hold. Even Dara was showing signs of frustration. Eventually 2 p.m. arrived, bringing with it the comfort that the jury would be back at work. I sat surrounded by everyone while we impatiently awaited news, any news. When three o'clock came I prayed that we wouldn't have to go through this again the next day. Court was due to end at 4 p.m., so it was not looking good. We were all coming to the devastating conclusion that we wouldn't have an answer today.

I was sitting lost in my own thoughts when I realised that some of the group were making their way towards the door into the court. In my foggy mind the small ocean of people looked as if they were being pulled towards a metaphorical plughole. For a few seconds it didn't register with me what was happening. I heard excited voices all around me but I couldn't make out what they were saying, and then Dara appeared in front of us. 'Gail,' he said, 'the verdict is in.' In that instant I felt as though I had been kicked in the back by a horse. The sudden pain in my lower back caused my legs to turn to jelly and I struggled to stand up. Barry and Dara helped me but as I reached the small hallway leading to the courtroom, I almost collapsed onto the floor. I couldn't breathe and had to be held up. As each person passed me, they offered words of comfort but I was unable to make out what they were saying because the sound of my heart thumping was deafening. Eventually I gathered enough strength to enter the room but had to be assisted to my seat.

The room was in chaos, with reporters rushing around trying to get ready to type the news story of the day. I could see my family and friends were a mess. Up to this point, I had managed to compose myself in a relatively calm and dignified way but that had all gone out the window now. I was more terrified than I had ever been in my whole life. Barry stood in front of me clutching my two trembling hands and I kept repeating, 'I can't do this, I can't do this.' There were tears streaming down both our faces.

From the other side of the room the clerk bellowed, 'All rise,' as Judge McCartan came in to take his seat. As Barry left me to go back to his seat, the judge instructed the clerk to summon the jury. One by one they walked into the room, their heads bowed. To me they all looked as if they were about to deliver the worst news imaginable for me. For the first time since my trial began I sat forward in my chair, clasping my shaking hands. I leaned on the small wooden shelf in front of me for support. A heavy silence fell throughout the room. After what felt like an eternity, the clerk asked the forewoman to stand. She said, 'Have you, the jury, reached a verdict?' The forewoman replied, 'Yes, we have.' She handed the clerk a sheet of white paper to read. The clerk took it, faced the court and read aloud, 'We, the jury, find the defendant Gail O'Rorke not guilty.'

The courtroom erupted. The strength once needed to endure this ordeal evaporated and all I could do was cry and cry. Nearly everyone was weeping. Barry, Dawn and Aaron had tears streaming down their cheeks and I could see them being supported by everyone around them. The once-composed group of staunch supporters officially lost their ability to keep a lid on it. As I looked towards the jury, I locked eyes with the forewoman who was now smiling from ear to ear. I mouthed the words 'thank you,' to which she nodded in recognition and smiled even more. For a wild moment I wanted to jump from my box, run over and kiss every one of the jurors.

Court was still officially in session, so we knew we had to attempt to behave in a dignified manner while the judge took charge of the room. Firstly he addressed the jury, sincerely thanking them for their service. He told them that owing to the difficulties associated with such a trial, they were excused from jury duty for the next ten years. As the six men and six women of that truly amazing jury stood to leave, they were given a standing ovation. The relief on their faces was palpable as they almost danced from the room. The big door closed behind them for the last time, and Judge McCartan turned to me. He said the words I had prayed endlessly to hear: 'Mrs O'Rorke, justice has been served here today. You have been found not guilty. You are free to go.' I stood up, ran towards Barry and out of the court, struggling to control my screams of happiness. Then Aaron and Dawn were with us, both of them in tears. We held on to each other in disbelief, crying uncontrollably.

They were followed by the court crew whose previously restrained emotions were now flowing like a river of tears of joy. I kept saying, 'Is this really over?' The constant crippling worry of the past few years had finally ended but my mind couldn't fathom that it was true.

After everyone eventually composed themselves, we had some breathing space in which we could try to calm down a bit. Dara, with a warm smile on his very relieved face, asked us to accompany him to a room to meet with the rest of the team. You could see on all their faces that they were ecstatic with the result. Barry was in such a state that Diarmuid jokingly told him to man up and stop crying. They went on to explain that the media were bursting at the seams to have an interview with me but the team advised me to write a statement instead, which would be copied and given to different reporters. As much as I knew that this was the best option, there was a big part of me that wanted to run towards the waiting cameras hand in hand with Barry, shouting from the rooftops that I was a free woman. However, I knew that my legal team knew best, so we sat for about twenty minutes while putting together a statement. The atmosphere in the small room was electric. They seemed almost as happy as I was with the result. They had worked tirelessly for so long, in ways I couldn't even imagine, to save me from conviction and now they could not get the smiles off their faces. How was I ever going to thank them?

When we were finished, we returned to our eager group. Aisling gave my statement to the waiting reporters and we all made our way to the ground floor. From where we stood, you could see out to the steps leading from the building. There were so many people waiting for us that again my nerves threatened to get the better of me. As we waited to settle ourselves for a few minutes, a reporter approached us. She had my statement in her hand and told Dara that they were reporting for the television and so a handwritten statement was useless to them. She was quite determined, but Dara calmly pushed his face towards her and sternly said, 'Tough!' before turning his back on her. Then he looked at me and said, 'This is your moment, not theirs.'

As we walked towards the door, Diarmuid gave me a big squeezy hug and a kiss on the cheek. This man, who only ever showed solemnity and professionalism, allowed his softer side to appear, even if only for a few seconds. Dara expressed his surprise, saying that it was the first time he had ever seen Diarmuid hug anyone. I felt honoured. With much trepidation we took our last steps from the Criminal Courts of Justice and left through the all-too-familiar double doors. There were countless cameras and microphones poised at the ready.

Every day up until that day we had always turned to our left to go up Infirmary Road, and clearly the media anticipated this route today, as did I. But as we stepped out, Barry tugged on my arm, dragging me off to the right towards where Aaron was waiting in the car. There was a panicked frenzy as reporters realised what was happening and they all ran after us, cameras in tow to get a comment or statement. It was crazy and wonderful all rolled into one. Barry opened the back door of the car and almost threw me onto the back seat. Cameras were pushed up against the windows as photographers and cameramen tried to get a picture. Most of what happened next is a blur because I am sure I was in shock and not focusing on anything except getting away.

About half a mile up the road Aaron pulled in. Our getaway driver was no longer needed and he left us to get into Laura's waiting car. Barry took over the reins and we were finally alone. Both of us broke down in tears. I don't think either of us could believe that the horror had ended and as much as we had shared our journey with so many people, only he and I truly understood the gravity of what had taken place. It was something that for so long had soaked into every thought, every bright day. The very thing that ate into every happy moment for so long was over now and we struggled to believe that those dark days had come to an end. No longer did I have to fear leaving my children and grandchildren. Never again did Barry have to fear living a life with a wife behind bars while trying to hold it all together for our little family. There had been a weight dragging us all down for what felt like an eternity and when the words 'not guilty' were uttered, the chain attached to that weight was severed, leaving us lighter and freer than we had felt for years. I also knew in my heart that for the first time since Bernadette had died, she was smiling down on us and was finally able to rest in peace. I thanked her for all that I believed she had done, because, although I had sat on my own in that little wooden box, I never felt completely alone because Bernadette was always by my side.

Epilogue

When I began writing this book, I always envisaged the story coming to an end once my trial was over. I imagined getting back to normal, returning to the life I had known. On reflection, I came to realise that life hadn't been normal for a considerable length of time.

In hindsight, I can now see how my stress levels had been increasing exponentially over the years. They would have begun when I started caring for Bernadette more as her illness worsened. Added to that was the struggle to help piece back together the splinters of Bernadette's life after the mess our car crash had left her in, as well as my own post-crash physical and emotional hurdles. Then there was the enormous stress of witnessing and helping her in shutting down her life, along with playing an integral role in her plans for a dignified death, the years of garda interviews and accusations, eventually being charged, all culminating in a trial filled with fear, doubt and mental torture. It amounted to many years of my life not really being 'mine', so thinking everything would just slot back into place was naive and unrealistic. It also should be noted, if I'm brutally honest, that I didn't want it to. Bernadette's journey, although personal and seemingly isolated, was something I didn't want to have been in vain.

As a highly intelligent, educated, independent and strong woman, she never should have had to face such struggles and barriers to achieve something that was no one else's business but hers. If she hadn't been disabled, her freedom of choice would have been significantly less infringed. It was her unavoidable need to rely on others for help that caused the rolling stone to gather so much moss that it became the mess it did for all involved. This final chapter covers the year after my trial and what effects, both good and bad, it had on me.

It begins with two very emotional and almost broken people travelling together away from the Criminal Courts of Justice, breathing in the air of the freedom we had dared to only dream about for so long. As Barry drove, we turned on the radio to listen to the news reports about my acquittal. We were both clearly still in a state of shock, struggling to absorb that it was all really over. We drove back to our house where we were going to get changed out of our uncomfortable clothes for the last time. Arrangements had been made to meet everyone in the Kiltipper pub for celebratory drinks. My phone was hopping with all the messages of congratulations coming through. When we arrived at the house, our usually busy little road was quiet, so we sneaked through our door and fell into each other's arms. We must have stood there for ten minutes just holding on in disbelief.

We changed and jumped back into the car to go and celebrate what was the best of days. When we drove into the car park of the pub, my brother-in-law Liam was standing in the doorway but he quickly vanished as soon as he saw us. When we walked into the lounge, the place erupted with cheers and clapping. It was a fantastic reception; everyone was as high as a kite. They were holding up a big sign my mad brother Paul had made earlier. On which was written, 'Proud to be a Gailette'. Everyone had signed it with their own little message for me. We were almost smothered with hugs. Gradually, word spread around the pub and before long everyone knew who we were. The entire court crew was there, the very people who had stood by us through thick and thin, who forfeited time, money, energy and lots of tears to help us through an ordeal that would almost have killed us if it hadn't been for them. These were the ones who watched us go from highs to lows, and who answered their phones at all hours simply because we needed them. Our children, who had endured so much heartache and upset, all the while staying strong for us; their partners, Adam and Laura, who took care of everything at home so our children could be with us, and for the many days they themselves came to court to support our family. My beautiful big sister Linda, who almost went under with the stress of watching me go through such a traumatic ordeal. Her husband Liam, who has always been a tough old codger and whose emotions had overflowed uncontrollably from the start. My three amazing brothers, Dave, Steve and Paul, and their partners Sheila, Ann-Marie and Anna, with their constant comfort, support and words of wisdom. My nieces, nephews, friends, cousins, aunts and uncles, each one having a huge role to play. Standing surrounded by all these truly amazing people made me feel joyous and blessed. No matter what the circumstances, they had reinforced a pride in me which was hard to put into words. And there in the pub I thought of my parents. They may have made a mess of parenting, but their actions throughout the years taught me to fight for what is right and just. If one single cog had turned in the slightest of ways, my path through life would have been a very different one and, I would imagine, a lot less eventful. Added to this, I share their love for the English language, one of the few positive things they reinforced throughout my childhood, and for these genetic and learned traits I will always be grateful. Never, no matter how petrified I was over the past few years, did I regret any of my actions; not one tiny detail would I have changed, and here I was now surrounded by the very best type of human beings imaginable. I simply could not have felt luckier.

About an hour after we arrived at the pub, the RTÉ news was on the television and the barman turned up the volume so everyone could hear it. It was quite funny watching the photographers and reporters panicking and running after us when we changed direction outside the court. I heard myself saying I was over the moon with the result, words I have no memory of uttering. When the news ended, everyone in the pub cheered and clapped. It was one of the best nights of our lives and we soaked up every last minute.

Sadly, there was one very vital person missing from our group. Tom Curran was unable to make it. There was a palpable void without him there. The stress of the trial and the years building up to it had taken a huge toll on him. In this life you meet many great people but Tom was in a category all his own. Without him, I would never have had Dara representing me. The ripple effect of Dara was meeting Diarmuid, Anne, Lorna, Lisa and Aisling, who with their combined levels of utter genius and tenacity saved me from the clutches of the prison system. Without Tom's willingness to share information with Bernadette, she would have had to face years of enduring the very horrors and indignities she had striven to avoid. I doubt Tom will ever truly comprehend his value in this world and it saddened me deeply that he couldn't be with us to celebrate our great news.

After many rounds of drinks, it was time for us all to return to our long-ignored and practically abandoned homes. Hugs and tears were in abundance as we parted ways. Before long I was in my PJs, watching telly with my best friend in the comfort of my living room. That night I slept the sleep of a free woman whose brain had been wiped clean of all the darkness it had become so accustomed to and I drifted off into peaceful bliss with hardly a worry in the world.

When I woke the next morning, for the first twenty seconds I forgot to not worry. Then, for the first time in a long time, I didn't lie staring at the bedroom ceiling. Instead, I jumped from my bed with a spring in my step and a head filled with happy thoughts.

Barry made me my usual delicious sweet cup of tea and we sat chatting, smiling and laughing, lapping up every moment of our first official morning of freedom together. We sat for about an hour before beginning our day. I walked into my living room and pulled up the blinds. When I looked across the road, there was a car parked on the corner opposite our house. Two people were sitting in the front seats, one of whom was holding up quite a large camera which was pointed directly at our home. I thought to myself, *Surely it's not the media*? But it was! They were reporters. I called Barry to come and have a look. We both became a little annoyed at the situation, so I pulled down the blinds and returned to the kitchen. Stupidly I had assumed that the media's interest would have stopped at the end of my trial, but that was a little naive on my part.

While we were sitting in the kitchen there was a knock at the front door and when I answered a reporter was standing there. He introduced himself, explaining that he was from the *Irish Daily Star* newspaper and asked if I would like to do an interview. I politely declined, briefly telling him that Barry and I were heading to a hotel for a few days on a short break. We spoke for two or three minutes before he thanked me for my time, explaining that he understood my request for privacy, shook my hand and left. All the while the other two reporters were still sitting in their car across the road. What could I do? They weren't breaking any law, so we stayed in for the rest of the afternoon in the hope that they would lose interest and go home.

The following morning the tiny bit of information that I did give at my front door was enough for the *Daily Star* to print a two-page article. I found it quite funny really. After a bit of breakfast we packed a few things and headed for the Clyde Court Hotel in Ballsbridge. It was exactly what the two of us needed. No reporters, no hassle, just a few days to unwind and relax. We didn't set foot outside the place for two days, staying in our room and leaving only to go to the restaurant for dinner. It was bliss. Early on our third day there I had a phone call from Linda asking would we mind if she and her family joined us. If I'm honest, I was a little disappointed because I wanted it just to be the two of us, but my sister wasn't taking no for an answer. She kept saying that they had a gift which my nephew and godson Barrie, who lives with his partner Dominique in Poland, had sent and that it had to be delivered straight away. We arranged to meet in the lobby an hour later. When they arrived, we sat and ordered a round of drinks, and then Liam realised that he had left the gift in the car and went to get it.

My curiosity was getting the better of me. I kept thinking it was something perishable. When Liam walked back in I could clearly see the urgency. The gift from Poland was my gorgeous nephew Barrie standing in the doorway with a great big smile on his beautiful face. It was a wonderful surprise and I jumped up and wrapped my arms around him. I hadn't seen him in so long. We have always been very close, but because of work commitments he had been unable to attend my trial. I was overjoyed to see him and we spent the next few hours catching up on all that had happened. He explained how devastated he was at not being able to come home. He was starting to build a new life for himself in Poland with a new job and couldn't take time off. He clearly felt guilty but I assured him there was no need. They all left a couple of hours later and Barry and I went back to the comfort of our room, where we cuddled up and watched a movie.

When we returned home from the hotel, we were delighted to find that there were no reporters outside the house. There were lots of flowers and cards on the front step from friends and neighbours, which was a really beautiful sight. Later that day, when we were out food shopping, we noticed that some newspapers were still printing articles about my trial and the general subject of assisted suicide. A couple of radio stations were also discussing it. I had previously made the decision to keep my head down and not do any interviews, but I was beginning to feel agitated listening to everyone discussing me when I couldn't respond. I decided to contact Susan Mitchell from the *Sunday Business Post*. About a year before my trial she and I did an article together on assisted suicide but, owing to my legal situation, it had to be written anonymously. Susan treated the matter with such respect. I felt relaxed in her company and trusted her implicitly to print the whole truth, so I contacted her and arranged to meet.

We met in Bijou restaurant in Rathgar the following day, directly across from Rathgar Travel from where the gardaí had taken me in for questioning on that fateful day. Susan and I sat together and talked openly about all that had happened. She discreetly placed a voice recorder on the table between us so that all the details would be correct. When we'd finished, she asked if I would accompany her across the road to the grounds of Rathgar church to have a few photographs taken as they wanted one to accompany the article. At no point while the interview was being recorded did I feel it was the wrong thing to do. I felt it would give me an opportunity to clear up any discrepancies that might have appeared in the public prints. We parted ways with Susan promising to email me a copy to read before she would send it to print. It might sound strange, but our meeting felt like a little counselling session. For the past few years I had been programmed to keep my mouth shut for fear that anything I said might affect my defence, but now, as a free woman, I could talk openly and it felt fantastic. Two days later the *Sunday Business Post* printed an article to be proud of. I was delighted with my decision and rang Susan immediately, thanking her from the bottom of my heart for doing such a wonderful job.

Over the coming weeks things at home settled down to almost normal with the exception of a few phone calls and texts asking if I was interested in doing interviews or articles with various media sources. One of these requests came from an assistant of Miriam O'Callaghan. She told me that they were doing a *Primetime* special on the subject of assisted suicide and wondered if I would be interested in coming on the show. After talking to Barry and checking with Dara, I said I would be delighted to. I didn't want Bernadette's journey to have been in vain and I really wanted people to see the human side of the tragic story and, more importantly, I wanted to highlight the subject as often as I could.

Barry and I travelled to the RTÉ studios in Donnybrook where we met Miriam and a colleague in the canteen. We went over what kind of questions she would ask. She is such a lovely woman, much taller than I expected, and is as beautiful in real life as she is on the screen. We had a great chat about all that had happened. I was relieved to feel so comfortable in her company and figured it would help when it came to being on live television. She gave me her word that she wouldn't ask me anything we hadn't discussed. I'm aware that some interviewers may do that to get a reaction but I didn't want Miriam to do that to me. The show was to air the following evening, so it was back again the next day to have my makeup and hair done. Tom Curran came with us, as did Dawn. I was chuffed that she accompanied me; I wanted to show her off because she is one of my greatest achievements in this life. Besides, I knew she would help to keep me calm.

My mind was awash with panic. I was going on live TV. What if I froze? Worse again, what if I swore, God knows the odd curse word slips from everyone's mouth occasionally. But everything went according to plan. Miriam kept her promise, asking only the questions we had discussed. It was wonderful being free to talk about my friendship with Bernadette. I wanted viewers to know our story and to tell anyone suffering or struggling with illness or disability that they were not alone in their worries and predicament.

Two days later Tom and I appeared on *Ireland AM*, a breakfast show hosted by Mark Cagney and Sinead Desmond. I was again really nervous, but having Tom sitting on the couch beside me sharing the limelight was great. I am always so in awe of Tom. When he speaks, he sounds so well informed and confident. I know he wouldn't agree, because he is way too modest to accept such a compliment. I felt we made a great team; both of us were so passionate about the right to die with dignity and taking every opportunity to encourage people to open their minds to those who wanted to have that choice. The idea that one should be allowed to end one's own life was new to people's minds. Suicide had been such a dirty word in Ireland for as long as I could remember but this type of suicide was completely different.

Watching the struggle Bernadette had to go through when she had clearly carried more than she could bear in the last months of her life tore my heart in two. It left me feeling so angry. Her plans to go to Dignitas should never have been stopped; it was her choice – a long-thought-through decision and an option which kept her from going insane during her darkest days. She knew that she would be able to escape the horrific existence her disease was forcing her to endure. It was her security blanket, and the authorities took this from her without ever considering what they were inflicting upon her. They didn't even show her the respect to call to her home to talk to her about it. They got to her through me, leaving a huge mess which they never even acknowledged. Stopping her plans to travel left this determined, desperate woman no option but to break the law by importing an illegal and banned substance into the country. Then she was forced to be sneaky, all the while being utterly terrified that this last option wouldn't work properly, thus leaving her in a vegetative state, which would lead to her being committed to some form of care home which she strove endlessly to avoid. So, honestly, how could I go quietly back to my normal life? I couldn't, and I was happy to sit with Tom, the staunchest of advocates on this subject. To bring about change, sometimes you have to make a lot of noise, and with each passing day I was determined to do something Bernadette never got to do. If she was in my position, she would have shouted about it from the rooftops, but she wasn't here, so it was my job to do my very best and get people thinking and talking about the subject openly.

Not long after our appearance on *Ireland AM* Tom and I were invited by Independent TD John Halligan to come to the Dáil to meet with other TDs. Tom and John, along with a team of barristers, had been working on a bill called the Dying with Dignity Bill where they proposed to bring forward legislation that would allow terminally ill people to have a physician-assisted death. It is a highly controversial subject but of great importance to many citizens in our country. We met with many independent TDs who were very much in support of the legislation. Unfortunately, there were no members of the larger political groups there to show their support. When leaving Leinster House, we were interviewed by RTÉ reporters, and this was aired on the news that evening. In general we felt the more publicity, the better.

A week later Tom rang, inviting me to attend one of Exit International's workshops which was to be held in Bewley's Hotel in Ballsbridge. Since Bernadette's involvement with Exit International I had been more than a little curious about these workshops and I agreed without hesitation. Barry, Dawn and Linda came with me. Tom asked if I would say a few words about my experiences over the past few years and talk a little about Bernadette's story. Philip Nitschke and his partner Fiona were hosting the workshop. When we arrived, Fiona was at the door to the function room, acting like a security guard and ensuring that only people who were on the list were to be allowed in. Tom later explained that sometimes members of the media tried to gain access and weren't always welcome. We looked around the room and noticed that there were one or two journalists attending who had obviously obtained permission.

Dotted around the room were several people who looked quite ill. One lady was gathering information on behalf of her husband, who was too sick with a terminal illness to attend himself. I sat nervously at the top table alongside Tom and Philip, listening intently to all they spoke about before reading the few lines I had prepared the day before. I am not going to go into detail about what took place because it is confidential and I don't want to disrespect the valued privacy Exit International holds so dear. What I will say is that it was very informative and for those in the room who wanted the choice to end their suffering, this information was beyond priceless. In the room with us were two young men who were making a documentary. They had been shadowing Philip and Fiona for several months. When the workshop ended, they approached me and asked if I would be interested in taking part in the documentary. I was very pleased and agreed to meet them the following day in town. I was delighted to have another opportunity to tell our story. I didn't really know what to expect, but I was willing to oblige.

When it was all over, Barry and Dawn headed home while Linda and I went out for dinner with Tom, Philip and Fiona. We went to a lovely French restaurant in town. Philip and Fiona are two amazing people who work tirelessly in the pursuit of a fairer world for terminally ill people looking to end their suffering. We had a great laugh; it felt as though we had known each other for years. And, as for the company of Tom, he has become one of my favourite people on the entire planet and I am now honoured to call him my very close friend. It was a lovely evening full of laughter.

The following afternoon Barry and I made our way to St Stephen's Green to meet with the documentary-makers. We were a little early, and, standing around, my nerves started to get the better of me again, but before long the men arrived and it was time to get to work. The place was packed with shoppers and tourists, who stared at us standing alongside two men with a huge camera and all the sound equipment. They wired me up with a microphone and briefly went over the way they wanted it to go. I walked around while the cameraman walked in front filming and the other young man walked beside me asking me questions about my journey with Bernadette. I started off feeling quite anxious, not helped by everyone stopping to stare at us, but before long, I relaxed. Barry walked ahead, clearing a path amongst the people so we could have an uninterrupted walk. It took about an hour to complete. We were all happy with how it went and we headed back home, once again delighted to have another opportunity to share my story.

At home, things had ever so slowly begun to return to normal. One of the things I haven't mentioned, and one of the happiest things to happen amongst all the worry and stress, was that Aaron and Laura were expecting another baby. By now she was almost four months' pregnant, but there were difficulties and she had to attend the Coombe maternity hospital regularly to be monitored. With every scan we all feared the worst, but the new life growing inside her seemed determined to hold on tight. Laura was forced to give up work as a hairdresser because it was no longer safe for her to stand for long periods. Bed rest was recommended but with two-year-old Baylee running around, it was almost impossible. Towards the end of July she began to lose her amniotic fluid, which brought concerns to a whole new level. In the first week of August she had lost nearly all the water surrounding the baby and had to be hospitalised.

Laura was only five months' pregnant and was now experiencing regular and intensifying pains. She was told that she wasn't in labour but Laura knew her own body and exactly what it was doing. It was difficult to watch how terrified she was of losing her baby, but there was nothing she could do except rest and try to hold on for as long as possible. After three long, painful days in hospital and sixteen weeks too early, her little man decided it was time to join us. Laura was rushed down to the labour ward and gave birth half an hour later. At precisely 11.16 a.m. on 12 August 2015 Arlo Ethan Aaron O'Rorke was born, weighing a tiny 700 grams. Barry and I were waiting in the parents' room when we received a photo of a tiny pink little baby. He was wrapped in plastic wrap, often applied to premature babies to reduce heat loss. Because he was a breech birth, his legs were still up at his shoulders. He looked so small and vulnerable. He was rushed to the neo-natal unit in intensive care and placed on a ventilator because his little lungs couldn't breathe on their own. It was a terrifying time for all of us, but Aaron and Laura were like two machines on automatic. Watching two people who to me were still only babies themselves taking care of something so tiny was awe-inspiring.

The first few days of Arlo's life were touch and go. He was called a micro-preemie, which is the smallest of premature babies. I remember being present when one of the doctors came to visit Laura a day or two before she gave birth. He explained that the hospital really treat a foetus as viable only once the mother has reached the twenty-four-week mark; anything earlier than that and there isn't a lot they can do to save the baby. Arlo was born on the first day of the twenty-fourth week. He held on in his mammy's tummy right until he knew he would be safe. He was a little miracle, with fingers thinner than a matchstick. If you had been allowed to hold him he would have fitted into the palm of your hand.

When he was two days old, he developed a blood infection, having no developed immune system. This was very worrying news. Close family members were called to the hospital and Arlo was christened while we all stood crying around his incubator, convinced that he wasn't going to make it. Watching his tiny little chest going up and down while a machine breathed for him was one of the toughest things I have ever had to witness. None of us really knew what to do; all we did was pray to whatever god we believed in and begged our angels to come down and protect this little fighter. Over the next twenty-four hours our prayers were answered because Arlo kept breathing. After a couple of worry-filled weeks, he was strong enough to be moved from intensive care to the high dependency unit, but within days he required surgery on his eyes, so he was moved back to the ICU. He remained on the ventilator, which in itself brought many problems. The longer a baby is on a ventilator, the more damage is done to the lungs and voice box, and Arlo had developed chronic lung disease, but for now the ventilator was the only thing keeping him alive.

After one hundred days of the most consuming worry imaginable, Arlo got another infection, which required him to have a lumbar puncture. The nurses placed him in isolation to reduce the risk of him picking up another bug. To our great relief, and with the help of the gods, he won the battle and was returned to the high dependency unit once again. Arlo was slowly gaining weight and this almost transparent mini-human being was beginning to look like a healthy little baby. He was taken off the ventilator many times in the hope that his lungs would work on their own, but every time he struggled to breathe and had to be intubated again, but eventually we received the miracle we had prayed endlessly for, as Arlo began breathing alone and unaided. Looking at the monitor beside his cot and reading the words 'not ventilated' was one of the best moments of our lives. After many days of fear, anxiety and hours upon hours spent sitting by his cot, two scared parents brought their miracle baby home. I remember how afraid they were at leaving the sterile safety of the hospital ward, taking Arlo home, where, no matter how much you clean, there will always be germs which could seriously affect his health.

He came home, still on a small dose of oxygen, and for the first few weeks, no visitors were allowed to see him while his parents wrapped him in cotton wool. There were so many new things for them to learn but together they worked miracles, keeping their baby safe and healthy. Since then, there have been many hurdles to overcome: Arlo has partial hearing impairment, which will require him to wear hearing aids, and mild cerebral palsy. But as I write this we have since celebrated Arlo's first birthday, a day we prayed and longed for. Since birth he has jumped over any hurdles put in front of him and has excelled in ways we could only have dreamed of. He is one of the happiest babies I have ever known. Now and for ever he will be known as our little Superman.

With everything that had happened over the past few years, stress upon more stress, my beautiful big sister suggested that the two of us get away for a while. We booked a week's holiday in Bitez, a resort in Turkey, where Linda had gone with her husband many times in the past. She highly recommended it. I couldn't wait; the thoughts of a week away put a big smile on my face every day in the run-up to it. There was no better person to go away with than Linda. She never has an itinerary and goes with the flow, which was exactly what I needed. We headed off on 13 September and I had one of the best weeks of my life. Having no one and nothing to be responsible for was heaven; lying in the sunshine doing literally nothing all day, every day, was wonderful. Everything was perfect. Well, until the flight home, that is. I began having feelings of impending doom, but since I couldn't understand why, I put it down to a case of the holiday blues and tried to ignore it. Barry and Liam were waiting at the airport to collect us when we arrived back. Barry's big smiling face on the other side of the barrier should have made me feel happy to be home, but instead it made me feel worse. All I wanted to do was turn on my heels and get back on the plane again.

Over the next few days my negative feelings went from bad to worse and within two weeks I was unable to find any level of happiness. Not even my beautiful grandchildren, who have always brightened up my days, could put a smile on my face. I stopped getting dressed, choosing to stay in my pyjamas all day. It was as if one Gail went to Turkey and a completely different one came home. Every day was a combination of crying, trembling and overwhelming bouts of anxiety. My head was so wrecked. I had watched my mother for so many years having the same things happen to her and I loathed the fact that I was now experiencing them. It made me feel frail and very angry, which only exacerbated everything. My mind played games with my sane, rational brain and I began to convince myself that it was all Barry's fault. Obviously I had fallen out of love with him, what else could it be? Looking back, I know how silly that sounds but at the time it made perfect sense. I put him through the mill daily and it was causing serious problems for us. I felt as though I was losing a battle with my own mind and I hadn't a clue how to fix it because I didn't know what had broken it or that it was even broken.

I confided in a friend, Jenny, one day about all the crazy thoughts I was having. She could see I was at my wit's end. I have always been such a happy person, seeing the positive in everything around me, but now that person was somewhere hidden from my view. Jenny asked if I had been to see a doctor, which I hadn't. Why would I need to see a doctor? I wasn't sick. Ever so gently she suggested that I might be suffering from depression. I disagreed. What had

I got to be depressed about? All my worries were behind me now; my trial was over. Arlo was doing really well, so why on earth would I be down? She wouldn't let the subject go and made me promise that I would go to see my doctor as soon as possible.

Two days later I called to see Jim Clarke, my GP, someone I felt very comfortable talking to. Many years back I used to clean for him and his wife, so I knew him on a personal level too. Barry came with me and stayed in the waiting room, so I could talk alone with Jim. As soon as my backside hit the seat, I was in tears. Jim told me that even before I had opened my mouth, he could see in my eyes that something wasn't right. After about fifteen minutes talking to him, Jim diagnosed me with severe depression and post-traumatic stress disorder. I asked why everything had changed so drastically when I came back from my holiday.

He described what had happened to me in the best way he could. He said that it was like falling off a cliff. The week away had caused a tidal wave of stress from the past few years to surge forward and there was nothing now holding it all back. Up until the time I had gone away, there was always something or someone to keep my mind distracted, stopping it from truly focusing on what I had gone through. The week in Turkey brought my defences down, so allowing a shut door to open wide and in flooded everything, almost drowning me in the process. I sat listening to everything Jim was saying and, although the voices in my head were arguing with him, my rational side knew he was right. He prescribed me a low dose of an anti-depressant which I was to take every day. I made an appointment to see him again in two weeks.

I remember sitting in the car with Barry outside the pharmacy holding the tiny white tablet on the tip of my finger. I was so annoyed that I had to take it and I struggled to put in in my mouth. I was sobbing, firstly because it made me feel embarrassed and weak and secondly because of the problem I had with my mother's pill-popping all through my childhood. But I placed the pill on my tongue and, through the tears, swallowed it.

Although I know it's not the same for everyone – and people have different ways of dealing with whatever issues they face – in my case, the anti-depressants helped. Well, those and the passage of time, which is perhaps the greatest healer. Over the weeks and months that followed, I came back to myself, and regained my sense of joy in life. I will forever be indebted to my tenacious friend Jenny for not giving up when I initially resisted her advice.

As I sit writing these very words it is December 2016. Thankfully Barry and I are better than ever, my two incredible children are happy and healthy, and all three of my amazing grandchildren are growing up fast and continue to fill my life and heart with a love so strong that it actually almost scares me. The worries of the past are far behind me and my future is glowing brightly. For the first time in a long time I have true peace in my soul. I hope beyond hope that the ripple effect from the legal journey I went on will bring change to the laws governing assisted suicide in our country and that Tom Curran's bill before the Dáil will be passed by open-minded and compassionate leaders who may someday find themselves or someone they love in a position where they too might long for the right to a dignified death.

Acknowledgements

I would like to thank the following people for helping my book come to fruition:

My agent Jonathan Williams for his patience and guidance in putting me on the right road to becoming a published author; Nicola Sedgwick for her wonderful editing skills; Breda Purdue and all at Hachette Ireland, especially Ciara Considine whose care, attention to detail and numerous suggestions made this book so much better in so many ways. To Kieran Kelly for his legal reading. To Tom Curran for recommending

Hachette Ireland as my publisher. To my siblings and partners for their constant input on an almost weekly basis, be it with forgotten information which required clarity or simply their valued opinion. To my children for standing by me on the emotional roller coaster of writing this book. And finally, I want to pay the biggest thank you to my best friend, soul mate and all round everything, my husband Barry: for always being there to discuss the book's content, for the memories he helped me to recall, for keeping me strong when my writing made me feel weak – there is simply too much to list, but without him by my side on this writing journey it simply would not have been possible.

Over all, I want to thank Bernadette Forde, for her friendship, support, loyalty, guidance and never-ending love. For making me a better woman and human being. For her encouragement and ability to see the good in everything and everyone. For the dignity, humility and strength which she had in abundance. She was and always will be one of the brightest, most beautiful stars in my universe and I will forever be grateful for all that she was to me in my life.